A BAKER'S FIELD GUIDE TO
Christmas Cookies

DEDE WILSON

THE HARVARD COMMON PRESS

Boston, Massachusetts

THE HARVARD COMMON PRESS
535 Albany Street
Boston, Massachusetts 02118
www.harvardcommonpress.com

Printed in China
Printed on acid-free paper

The Library of Congress has cataloged the original edition as follows:

Wilson, Dede.
   A baker's field guide to Christmas cookies / Dede Wilson.
       p. cm.
   ISBN 1-55832-263-9 (hc : alk. paper)
       1. Cookies. 2. Christmas cookery. I. Title.
   TX772.W525 2003
   641.8'654—dc21

                                                            2003007484

Reprint ISBN: 978-1-55832-751-1 (pbk.)

Special bulk-order discounts are available on this and other
Harvard Common Press books. Companies and organizations
may purchase books for premiums or resale, or may arrange a
custom edition, by contacting the Marketing Director at the
address above.

Book design by Night & Day Design
Cover and interior photographs by Eric Roth Photography
Food styling by Mary Bandereck

10 9 8 7 6 5 4 3 2 1

This book is dedicated to

Mary McNamara, one of my best friends

and an excellent baker. Her lucky

husband and kids never know what

goody she might bake up on any given

day—but it is always delicious!

Contents

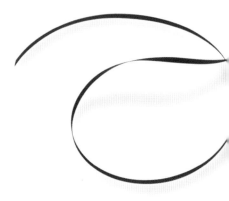

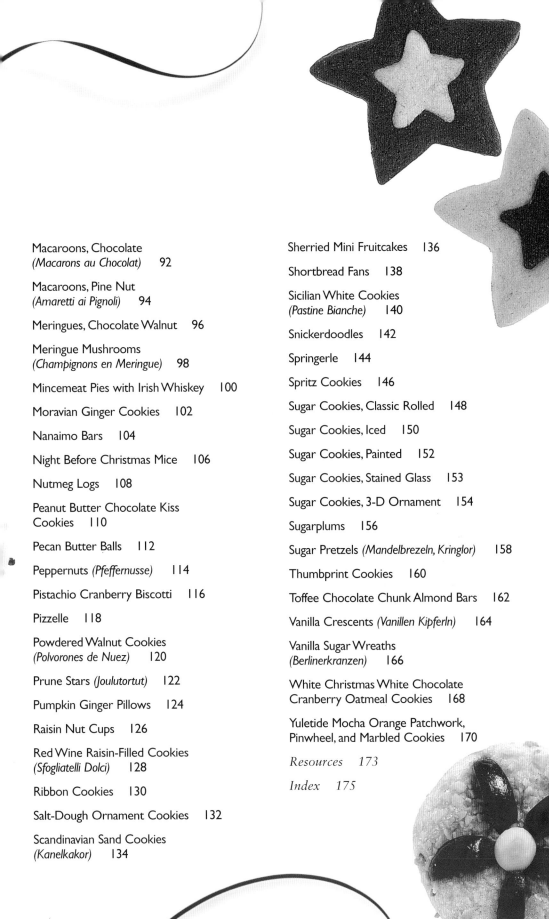

Acknowledgments

A big thank you to Pam Hoenig, who brought this project to me and gave me free reign to scour the world for delicious holiday cookies. Thanks also to Bruce Shaw, publisher of The Harvard Common Press, for giving me his stamp of approval.

This book is enriched by the recipes generously given to me by so many family members and friends: my dad, Moses Acosta, for assembling an international list of helpers; Robert Agro for his *struffoli*; Darina Allen from Ballymaloe Cookery School for her mincemeat recipe; Valerie Cimino for her family's Italian cookie recipes; Lou Currin for her help in researching southern recipes; Angie Czajkowski for her Polish recipes; Joan Eckert for her Swedish recipes; Nathan Fong for insight on the origins of Nanaimo Bars; Aglaia Kremezi for so promptly answering my questions about Greek holiday cookies; Carolyn Laychak for her help with the holiday pastries of Hungary; Beatrice Ojakangas for her Finnish prune pastries; Christopher Rivers for his family's many southern heirlooms; Christina Trivero for her decadent bourbon balls; and Naomi Waynee and her MilleniuM bull terriers for their dog biscuit recipe.

A big, special thank you goes to the staff at Kitchen Arts & Letters, especially Matt Sartwell. He was pressed into service more than once when I needed help with historical research. Matt is as quick and efficient as he is a joy to speak with.

Thank you to my agents, Maureen and Eric Lasher. This is book number five—who knew? You did! And you support me at every turn.

Mary McNamara is always there for me to discuss baking ideas and techniques and to test recipes. I will literally call her up and suggest a baking day and she is always accommodating, my house or hers. Mary helped brainstorm the "drop by generously rounded teaspoon" language and pointed out that most people would have thought me a bit nuts to dwell over such a topic, but she actually found it interesting! I have called her my baking muse in the past; she still is and always will be.

Thank you to Juanita, Tom, and Daniel Plimpton, who ate hundreds of these cookies. Now, Juanita and Tom think everything I bake is great, which is always nice to hear. On the other hand, their son, Daniel, is a budding food critic, always offering incredibly insightful feedback—and he has been doing so since he was ten! Daniel will nibble on one cookie for fifteen minutes, savoring every crumb, critiquing every morsel. Every baker dreams of having such an audience.

And, always, thanks to my partner, David Kilroy, and my kids, Ravenna,

Freeman, and Forrester, for indulging me during baking frenzies. Ravenna is off to college and I promise to send cookie care packages. Freeman and Forrester, you guys can count on me to bake for you anytime. And Beckett, the dog biscuits are for you!

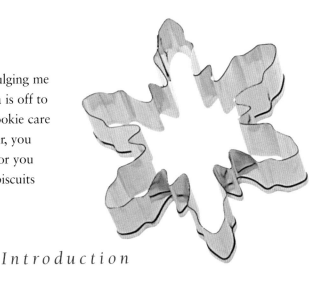

Introduction

My first cookie memory is from the age of four. My mom and I were making gingerbread people, and I decided the ginger-men and ginger-women should be anatomically correct. My mom thought that was great; my aunt, who was looking on, wasn't so sure. So some were embellished and some were not, but they were all given cinnamon red-hot candy eyes because I just love that combination of chewy gingerbread and the crunch from the spicy cinnamon candies.

Cookies were also the first dish I became "famous" for. They are the same ones as those described on page 96—a meringue cookie filled with semisweet morsels and chopped walnuts. I learned to make them when I was about eight; my mom and I found the recipe in a church cookbook put together by my school. It seemed easy enough. That is until my mom suggested we whip the egg whites by hand in a copper bowl. She took a turn with the balloon whisk, then me, then her, then me, and the egg whites still weren't stiff enough. It took us so long, and our arms

were so tired, that we decided to give the mixer a try next time. That made it a breeze and I started making the cookies for any and all occasions. The sweet meringue combined with the toasted walnuts and luscious dark chocolate is irresistible—and they go together in a flash. I memorized the recipe and made them on the spur of the moment at friends' houses, right up through my teens and into adulthood.

I have learned a lot about cookies since then; principally that there is the perfect cookie for every taste and that they are a joy to make. And as I mentioned above, they can make memories—sweet ones at that! Christmas is the perfect time of year for making cookies and memories with your family, so dig right in.

Most of these recipes are very easy, while some require a special mold or a little more attention. All of them, however, are easy to follow and will give you delicious results any time of year.

Happy Holidays and Merry Baking!

How to Use This Book

This is the first-ever Baker's Field Guide to Christmas Cookies! Every cookie has its own page with information indicating its Type (drop, rolled, molded, filled, etc.), its country of origin (Habitat), a Description of how that cookie tastes and looks, Field Notes on traditions or tips or interesting related bits of information, variations (Related Species), and how long they will keep (Lifespan). You will also find symbols for the following special characteristics under the recipe title:

Also, look to the end of the recipe for Good Cookie Tips for easy variations and specific information, where needed, that will help you make your cookies as good as they can be.

But first . . .

What Is a Christmas Cookie?

- They can be cookies with a seasonal shape, such as stars, bells, and reindeer
- Some feature holiday flavors such as peppermint, ginger, molasses, pumpkin, or cranberry
- They might keep well, so you can bake early and reap the rewards of extra time during the season
- Some are quick to whip up, because time is short during the holidays
- Others are extra fancy—because it's Christmas!

- Some doughs freeze well, for those who plan ahead
- Some have a history in a particular country and feature native spices and traditional shapes
- Others are particularly sturdy and great for mailing
- They can be cookies that are easy to make in large batches, so you'll have plenty to eat, give away, mail to friends, and have on hand for impromptu guests
- Some are tried and true, like cutout sugar cookies
- Some bring the excitement of the unexpected and a smile to your face (see page 106)

Ingredients

Here is a short list of ingredients you'll find in these recipes that you may be less familiar with or that I have tips for selection or use. Remember, if you start with high-quality ingredients, you'll get the best results.

SUGAR AND OTHER SWEETENERS: Of course, I use granulated and confectioners' sugar, but here are some other specialty sugars and sweeteners you might want to have around:

Coarse sugar: This is a crystalline coarse-grained sugar used to decorate some cookies. See Resources for information.

Colored sugars: Colored sugars are

9

used to decorate cookies and can be found in a variety of colors. See Resources.

Pearl sugar: This sugar also has a coarse texture, but it is an opaque white color. See Resources.

Nonpareils: These are sugar decorations, often multicolored. The type used in this book is a tiny ball the size of a head of a pin, and can be found in the supermarket.

Honey and molasses: Use orange blossom or wildflower honey and unsulfured molasses for these cookies. These can be sticky—and tricky—to measure. Lightly coat the inside of your liquid measuring cup with nonstick spray, then pour in the desired amount of liquid sweetener. It will then slip right out.

MILK, CREAM CHEESE, SOUR CREAM: Use full-fat varieties.

HEAVY CREAM: Use cream labeled "heavy" as opposed to "whipping" for best results. Heavy cream has a higher butterfat content.

EXTRACTS: Use pure vanilla and almond extracts.

CITRUS ZESTS: Make sure to use just the colored part of the zest and not the white pith.

CHOCOLATE AND COCOA: Use the best-quality chocolate and cocoa you can find and afford.

Morsels and chips: When recipes call for these, you can use the standard supermarket variety or cut your own bulk chocolate into ¼-inch pieces.

White chocolate: Look for white chocolate that lists cocoa butter in the ingredients and not palm or other oils. The cocoa butter will give it a chocolatey flavor and aroma.

Cocoa: Most all of these recipes call for Dutch-processed cocoa, so check the label. It should say "Dutch-processed" or "alkalized"; if it says "natural," that's not the right kind. You can find Dutch-processed cocoa in the supermarket. The natural-style cocoa, which is lighter in color, is used for contrast in the Kris Kringle's Chocolate Krinkles recipe (page 88). This too can be found in the supermarket.

Tempering chocolate for dipping cookies: Some of the cookies in the book call for a dip in chocolate after cooling, such as the Chocolate-Dipped Almond Drops (page 44). Other cookies, like Cherry Orange Florentines (page 38), have melted chocolate spread on the bottom. Either way, if the chocolate is tempered (which is simply melting it in a particular way, which stabilizes the fat crystals in the cocoa butter, which in turn prevents the chocolate from streaking after cooling), the results will be very professional looking. Tempered chocolate will stay glossy even without refrigeration. Start with the desired amount of chocolate as stated in the recipe and chop it very finely. Place about two-thirds of it in the top of a double boiler over gently simmering water. Stir gently to encourage melting, but do not stir vigorously, which will add air. As soon as the chocolate is melted, remove from the heat and wipe the bottom of the pot to eliminate any chances of water droplets reaching the chocolate, which would cause it to seize. Add about one-third of the chopped chocolate and stir gently. The residual heat will melt it. As soon as it is melted, add the remaining chocolate, in two more stages, continuing to stir gently until it is completely melted. It is now ready to use. To double check whether it is ready, dip your index finger into the chocolate and place a dab of melted chocolate on your lower lip; it should feel warm, but not hot. If it is too hot, stir in some more chopped chocolate. If you have an instant-read thermometer, place it into the chocolate; it should read between 89 and 91 degrees F (for dark chocolate, which is the only type tempered and used in this book). Please note that it is easiest to temper at least 8 ounces of chocolate, but many of the recipes call for less. The amount listed in the recipe is the amount you need for that specific recipe. Here is what I suggest: If you are baking two or more cookies that require tempered chocolate, consider making them on the same day so that you can temper one batch of chocolate, which will make your cookie baking process very efficient. Otherwise, consider tempering at least 8 ounces, and any unused can be allowed to harden; then you can chop it up and add to a batch of Toffee Chocolate Chunk Almond Bars (page 162) or fold it into ice cream.

NUTS: Make sure your nuts are fresh and haven't gone rancid. If not using right away, store them in the refrigerator or freezer.

Toasting nuts:

A number of recipes in this book called for toasted nuts. To toast and skin hazelnuts, spread them in a single layer on a cookie sheet and bake in a preheated 350-degree F oven until they begin to give off an aroma and the skins have turned dark brown and split, exposing the browning nut. This will take about 12 minutes. Shake the pan once or twice to encourage even browning. Remove from the oven and cool on a rack, then take clean kitchen towels and rub the nuts vigorously between them. With a little work, the skins will come off. My hazelnuts usually retain a tiny bit of skin on them; that's fine. Hazelnuts can be purchased peeled, at an added expense.

To toast almonds, walnuts, pecans, or pistachios, spread in a single layer on a cookie sheet and bake in a 350-degree F oven until they begin to give off an aroma and are light golden brown. This will take 5 to 10 minutes, depending on the nut and the amount. Shake the pan once or twice during toasting to encourage even browning. Remove from the oven and cool on a rack before using in a recipe. Always cool nuts before chopping. The oils, which will have been brought to the surface by the heat, must be reabsorbed or the nuts could turn greasy when chopped.

SPICES: All of the spices in the book, such as cinnamon and cardamom, are ground. However, several recipes call for freshly ground nutmeg. When freshly ground, nutmeg is very light and fluffy and the measurements are very different from pre-ground nutmeg. If you choose to use pre-ground, you will need less and should adjust to taste.

CANDIED FRUIT AND PEELS: Buy high-quality candied fruits and peels at a specialty store or through mail order.

FOOD COLORING: Liquid food coloring is available in supermarkets in basic colors, but many mail-order sources offer dozens of colors in formulations I prefer. Many professionals use paste, gel, and powdered colors, and these are what you will find at specialty stores and through mail order (see Resources).

Equipment

MIXER: I used a freestanding 5-quart KitchenAid mixer to test these recipes. If using a handheld mixer, the mixing times will be longer.

FOOD PROCESSOR: The recipes were tested with a KitchenAid 11-cup Ultra Power Food Processor. You will need a food processor with a metal blade to make these recipes.

COOKIE SHEETS: Most cookie sheets are flimsy, warp, and encourage burning. These recipes were tested with heavy-weight aluminum or stainless-steel rimmed cookie sheets (also called half-sheet pans or jelly-roll pans). Thinner sheets will more than likely brown cookies faster. But, and this is a big but, this is based on how these pans performed for me in my kitchen in my oven. Your oven might work symbiotically with another cookie sheet, so it is really up to you to experiment. In general, however, the heavier the cookie sheet, the better it is for even baking. Try doubling up your cookie sheets if you are getting burned bottoms. There are insulated cookie sheets available, but they often prevent cookies from suitably browning, which I do not find desirable.

PARCHMENT PAPER: Parchment is available in rolls, like aluminum foil, from kitchenware stores and supermarkets. I use it to line my cookie sheets to eliminate sticking. Parchment can also be cut into triangles to make paper cones. I use these for adding extra jam to linzer cookies and to write names on cookies for placecards.

PASTRY BAGS: Some of these recipes require pastry bags, fitted with various tips, for applying decorative icings or for piping out cookies themselves. I like the polyester type made by Wilton. They are called Featherweight Decorating Bags, and come in sizes ranging from 8 to 18 inches (in 2-inch increments). The openings are trimmed to allow a large decorating tip to fit, or to fit a coupler, which allows you to change small tips easily. I find the 14-inch-size bag to be the most convenient.

Decorating tips: Tips are quite inexpensive (usually less than two dollars), and owning a variety will allow you to experiment with different looks. Every tip has a number, but depending on the manufacturer, the numbers can vary. So I have given you tip numbers for the Ateco brand tips that I use as well as a description, such as "½-inch star tip" so that you can duplicate my instructions as closely as possible.

Decorator's comb: This is a very specialized tool, but it is also very inexpensive and can be mail-ordered from Sweet Celebrations (see Resources). It is a small, flat, triangular piece of metal or plastic; each edge has a different design, and you drag it through icing or chocolate (like on the bottoms of the Cherry Orange Florentines) to create a texture and pretty pattern.

Bench scraper: This is a rectangular piece of stainless steel with a wooden or hard plastic handle along one long side. I use it to gather ingredients together from my work surface, scrape up bits of dry ingredients, like chopped chocolate, spread batter into pans, and scrape my work surface clean after rolling out dough. But my favorite use is for cutting bars cleanly (see page 16, Recipe Yields and Cutting Bars).

Doubling and Halving Recipes

Since you will more than likely need an abundance of cookies at Christmastime, I have been generous in scaling the ingredients and most of the recipes will yield between 50 and 100 cookies. However, occasionally you might want more or less cookies than the recipe is scaled for. Many recipes can be halved, while most of the recipes are too large to double—a handheld mixer will not be able to handle the amount. In general, however, it is best to make the recipe as is, because sometimes the balance of ingredients is such that even halving or doubling them will wreak havoc with the results. I have tested the recipes as presented so you may increase or decrease them if you like, but it will be an experiment. I suggest that if you want only half of a recipe and the dough can be frozen (it will say in the individual recipe), then make the total amount, freeze half, and bake the rest, saving the frozen half for a later date. If you want double the recipe, use a large-capacity stand mixer and, again, know that the results might be different than what I had originally intended.

Freezing Cookie Dough

Cookie dough with a high butter content, such as that for Classic Rolled Sugar

Cookies (page 148), freezes well. To know which cookie dough can be frozen, look for the 🔖 symbol. Then, at the stage in the recipe where the dough requires chilling, double wrap the dough in plastic wrap, slip into a heavy-duty zipper-lock plastic freezer bag, remove all the air, and freeze for up to a month. Defrost dough in the refrigerator overnight, then proceed with the recipe. Make sure to label your dough or you might end up with unidentifiable cookie dough masses scattered about your freezer! I like to freeze small batches so that I can whip up freshly baked cookies even when time is short.

While many bakers like to freeze cookies after baking, I prefer not to, as I think they always taste less than fresh (there are a couple of exceptions in the book, and specific instructions are given within individual recipes). If you would like to experiment with freezing baked cookies, your best bet is to try to freeze the same types of cookies that have freezer-friendly dough (just look for the symbol). After the cookies have cooled completely, package them in airtight plastic containers, separating the layers with waxed paper. Fill up the containers so there is very little air space, slip into a heavy-duty zipper-lock plastic freezer bag, and remove all the air. Freeze for up to a month, then defrost, still wrapped, until they come to room temperature. Do not freeze cookies that have powdered-sugar coatings or any type of frosting or sugar decoration, as they will be ruined during the deep-freeze storage.

Forming Cookies

For years I have read recipes that say "drop batter by teaspoonfuls," and when I took the time to think about it I realized I had no idea what they meant. If I actually measured a teaspoonful, it was much tinier than what was intended. If I took two teaspoons out of my utensil drawer (you know, the spoons you use to eat cereal with) and scooped up batter to drop on the cookie sheets, like most home bakers do, there was no uniformity or any way to really know how much batter I was doling out.

For accurate baking times and yield counts, I wanted to be more precise for these recipes. Many drop cookies end up being a generously rounded teaspoon in size, and I found an ice cream scoop (called a food disher) that not only facilitates measuring, but also allows quick scooping and dropping onto cookie sheets since it has a quick-release mechanism. If you want to duplicate my recipes as closely as possible, I suggest you get one of these. It is a Zeroll brand #100 scoop and is available through King Arthur Flour The Baker's Catalogue (see Resources). It will make many of these recipes go very quickly, and the tool is very easy to use. To use an ice cream scoop effectively for forming cookies, dip it into the batter, generously filling the bowl of the scoop. Scrape off the excess batter against the side of the bowl to form a level scoop, then drop directly onto the cookie sheet. Some of the recipes call for a generously rounded tablespoon and that measurement can be doled out with a Zeroll #40 scoop.

TIP: *My recipes will say "drop by generously rounded teaspoon." If you do not have one of the aforementioned scoops, the measurement is supposed to be about 1¾ teaspoonfuls. Feel free to scoop and drop batter any way you like, but actually measure out the first cookie so that you will then know how to measure out the rest by eye. Remember, if you use a different amount, your baking times, results, and yield will vary from those stated in the recipe. Same goes for recipes that say "drop by generously rounded tablespoon," in which case the measurement is about 1½ tablespoonfuls.*

If a stiff batter is to be rolled into a ball between your palms, I give you specific measurements and directions such as "roll dough between your palms into 1-inch balls." Actually measure the first cookie with a ruler; then you can roll the rest by eye.

When rolling out dough to cut with cookie cutters, there will be a thickness given, such as ¼ inch. It is a good idea to actually measure the thickness of the dough for accurate results.

Baking Times

Simply put, baking times are approximate and that is why every recipe says "bake about" a certain number of minutes. A visual description of the cookie is also given. Your oven might have hot spots and/or your cookie sheets might perform differently, so always check for doneness before the suggested baking time—and use those visual cues!

NUMBER OF PANS IN OVEN: Cookies need to have an even flow of heat and air all around them to bake as evenly and beautifully as possible. This is partially accomplished by spacing the cookies on the sheets as directed in individual recipes, but another important technique is to limit the number of pans in the oven at any given time. While most ovens have at least three racks, I find that baking one or two pans at a time gives the best results, and that is how I tested these recipes. If you crowd the oven, you might burn your cookies or, at the very least, get different and unexpected results. Because of this approach, the recipes call for a maximum of two cookie-sheet pans; you will need to reuse your pans a few times for most recipes. Always let pans cool before reusing.

ROTATING PANS HALFWAY THROUGH BAKING: To help your cookies bake as evenly as possible, another technique is to rotate pans front to back (and even between racks) at least once during baking. I have not added this direction to each recipe, as I am encouraging you to work it into your baking routine as a matter of course.

Proper Cooling

You might think the recipe is over once the cookies are out of the oven, but proper cooling is essential for a great final result. Some cookies will initially be cooled still on the pan set on a rack for a few moments before being transferred to the rack directly to cool completely. Others are removed from the pan immediately to instantly stop residual cooking through the heat of the pan. Follow the specific instructions given in a particular recipe. And always cool completely before placing in storage containers.

Recipe Yields and Cutting Bars

The recipes will have a yield number, which tells you how many cookies or bars you will get, if you follow my directions. For cookies that are rolled out, I tell you what size cookie cutter I use and the yield will say "fifty 3-inch cookies." Perhaps you want to use a cookie cutter of a different size. That's fine, but your yield will be different.

For bars, the recipe will say "cut into 16 bars (4 x 4)." This means that you divide the pan into horizontal rows of 4 bars by vertical rows of 4 bars to give you the suggested 16 bars. Bars can often be cut smaller or larger, which will alter your yield.

How to Bake Perfect Cookies

- Read every recipe through before starting
- Use the ingredients called for (for instance, do not substitute extra-large eggs for large)
- Take time to measure accurately with the proper tools
- Use the time cues and visual cues when mixing and baking for best results
- Do not overbake—I believe the number-one problem with baking cookies is overbaking
- Cool cookies properly
- Store cookies according to individual instructions
- Relax, and enjoy baking your Christmas cookies!

To cut bars, I definitely have a preferred method—using a bench scraper. Take the tool by the handle and press the sharp edge straight down into the bars; repeat to make a complete cut either across or down the length of the pan by lifting and pressing, lifting and pressing. If the bars are sticky, wipe the blade clean between cuts with a warm, wet cloth. Cutting in this fashion eliminates the bulk of the drag created by pulling a knife through a pan of bars; the edges will be cleaner and give you prettier results.

Storing Cookies

Cookies, whether soft, chewy, or crisp, will benefit from being stored in an airtight container—but not together! Crisp cookies will become limp if stored with soft ones, so make sure to have enough tins and airtight containers for all of your cookies. Also, make sure to cool cookies completely before placing in a storage container or the heat might create condensation.

There is a product called Blue Magic that helps crisp cookies stay that way. It is a small device a little larger than a walnut that has a clear glass bottom and perforated metal top. Inside is a dry chemical that absorbs moisture. You place one of these devices in your cookie jar and it absorbs any moisture so that crisp foods stay crisp. It is inexpensive and can be mail-ordered (see Resources).

For soft cookies, there is something called a Brown Sugar Bear, which is a small piece of terra-cotta shaped like a teddy bear. You soak it in water, then place it in a container with soft cookies to help retain their texture. You can also place it in a container of brown sugar to help keep it soft (see Resources).

Sending Cookies by Mail

A mailed gift package of cookies is always well received, but you want to make sure they arrive in as good condition as when they were cooling in your kitchen.

First, choose your cookies wisely. Some bar cookies make good choices for mailing, as do soft cookies without any soft frosting or icing. Firm, crisp cookies, such as shortbread, are a good choice too. Steer clear of lacy or delicate cookies, which break easily. Also, cookies that have shapes with pointed corners, such as stars, break easily too. Cookies that must be refrigerated or that have thick fillings are also best served at home. In individual recipes, I have pointed out with a special symbol ✉ which cookies I think survive the mailing process the best.

Begin by packing each kind of cookie in its own small tin or airtight plastic container. I go to the dollar store and load up. Make sure the shapes of the containers are large enough to allow cookies to lay flat on the bottom. Make a single layer of cookies, top with a piece of waxed paper cut to fit, and proceed to add layers of cookies, without overlapping cookies on any given layer. When they overlap, they are more prone to breakage. The last layer should be near the top of the container. Crumple plastic wrap and lay it over the top layer of cookies, then press the top of the container down onto the cushioned layer of plastic wrap. Gently shake the container; the cookies should not have any wiggle room. If there is still too much air space and the cookies are moving around, add more plastic wrap.

Once each of your different kinds of cookies is wrapped in its own container, place the various containers in a large sturdy box that has been partially filled with Styrofoam "peanuts" packing material, then top off with more peanuts before sealing the box. You want to fill up the outer box with peanuts so that the individual containers are as snug as possible and don't swim around in the box. Alternatively, tape all of the cookie containers together, wrap completely with bubble wrap so that the entire package fits snugly inside your outer box. You can also use crumpled newspaper in lieu of peanuts.

Millions of packages are mailed at Christmastime, so make sure to ask the postmaster how long it will take and plan accordingly. I usually figure extra money into my budget so that I can send my cookies overnight or, at the most, by two-day post. At the very least, I suggest mailing early in the week to minimize the chance of your cookies sitting in a warehouse over the weekend. You want your cookies to be as fresh as possible when they arrive.

Giving Cookies as Gifts

Homemade treats are always appreciated, and I think cookies are the best baked item to give. Why? Because they are simply there for your pleasure and make no demands. If you bring someone a cake, it usually must be served as soon as possible. Cookies are there for when you need them, such as when someone drops by unexpectedly, and for when you want them, whether with tea in the afternoon or as a late-night snack. During the holidays there are numerous occasions when cookies are simply the perfect treat to have.

The fact that you took the time to bake and have chosen a lucky recipient means that the bulk of your labor of love has been accomplished. But let's consider gift wrapping. With a little extra effort you can turn your cookies into an extra-special gift.

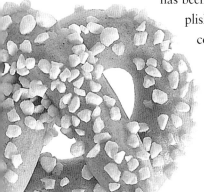

First of all, the cookies have to be in some sort of container that will keep them fresh, and decorative tins are my favorite way to go. Many dollar stores and discount stores, especially around the holidays, stock tins of all sizes. If you use these, which are usually quite colorful and often have holiday themes emblazoned upon them, all you need to do is add a big bow. Go to the fabric or craft store and buy wired ribbon. These are ribbons that have very thin wire running down the length of each side, which allows you to form gorgeous bows quite easily. I also like the dollar and discount stores for decorative bags. You can find very fancy shopping bags, from those tiny enough to hold one cookie to ones large enough to hold several dozen. In this case, you can place your cookies in simple plastic containers, then add colorful tissue paper or cellophane to the bag along with the cookie containers, for an elegantly packaged gift. These stores will have gift boxes, too. They are not airtight, so place simple plastic containers inside.

Scour flea markets for antique containers, which don't have to be expensive. Even something as recent as a 1950s, '60s, or '70s cookie jar can sometimes be found at a steal, as can tins from decades earlier. You can always find cheap, one-of-a-kind plates at flea markets. Arrange your cookies on one of these, then add colored plastic wrap and ribbon. Maybe you have never noticed, but right next to the regular plastic wrap in the supermarket, there is colored wrap—and they always have red and green during the holidays.

Think in terms of what you have around the house, too. Recycled crates, tins, wooden gift boxes, and baskets can all be put to use.

Once your packaging is done, whether it is a box, bag, or tin, you can add further embellishments. Thread a cookie cutter through the ribbon, or punch a hole in a recipe card and include that. You could also include the recipe card inside the tin, box, or bag. There are also some small tools, such as tiny whisks, that are inexpensive and look great perched on top of a present. Or consider using decorative labels to stick on packages that give the name of the cookie.

If you have a selection of containers, colored tissue paper, plastic wrap, and ribbons at hand, you will be able to put together a present-worthy gift of cookies in a flash.

Cookie-Exchange Parties

Nothing is better than a cookie tray filled with several varieties of cookies, especially when they are all homemade. But nobody ever said that you had to make all the cookies yourself! Organize a Cookie-Exchange Party, and you and your friends will all go home happy with dozens of cookies to share with your families and to have on hand during the busy holiday season.

Send out invitations asking guests to bring a large platter and several dozen of their favorite homemade cookies. A nice addition is to also have them bring photocopies of their recipe to hand out. Once your guests have assembled, everyone swaps cookies and loads up their platter with several cookies of each type. You provide beverages, such as mulled cider, and as many types of homemade cookies from your own kitchen as you like. Have plastic wrap on hand for wrapping up platters; the extra-wide wrap is particularly useful, and I suggest going to the dollar store to buy extra platters— a few extra are usually needed. Many cookies will be eaten on the spot, but that just adds to the fun.

Cookie-Decorating Parties

Another type of cookie party is the Cookie-Decorating Party. This is especially popular with kids and can be a great birthday party activity if your child's birthday falls during the holiday season. However, do not limit it to the younger set; cookie decorating has a way of bringing out the child in all of us. Send out invitations asking each guest to bring his or her imagination and a sense of adventure.

Bake up large batches of Classic Rolled Sugar Cookies (page 148) and Gingerbread People (page 72), all devoid of decoration. Use various cutters such as men, women, Santas, Christmas trees, reindeer, and such so that there is a wide selection. Clear a large table and set the cookies in the middle along with as many different decorations as you like. I suggest at least half a dozen colored sugars, cinnamon red-hot candies, silver and gold *dragées*, nonpareils, miniature M&Ms, miniature chocolate chips, and chocolate and rainbow sprinkles. Then look in the baking aisle of the supermar-

ket and load up on the kind of icing that comes in a tube; get the plain white as well as red, green, yellow, and blue. Also buy the little package that has decorating tips that screw right onto the tube frosting; this makes decorating cookies a breeze. You can also find gel frostings, which are translucent; buy a few of those, too. A newer product that is readily available is an edible colored spray. This gives a unique effect, and you might want to give it try; look for it right alongside the frostings in the supermarket.

Once your ingredients and guests are assembled, get the party going by grabbing a cookie, applying some frosting, and adding the dry decorations on top, where they will stick to the frosting. Invite everyone to jump in, kids and adults, and make the point that perfection is not the goal. Let creativity rule!

The
Field Guide

Almond Cream Cookies
Mandel Moussla

❋ **TYPE** *Molded cookie*   ❋ **HABITAT** *Sweden*

❋ **DESCRIPTION** *This cookie, which is actually a tiny pastry, has several components. There is the soft-crumbed, almond-flavored cookie itself, which is baked in miniature muffin tins. After they cool, they are topped with whipped cream and a dollop of preserves for quite an elegant look. Unlike many cookies that have so many parts, these cookies are actually delicious without their embellishments.*

❋ **FIELD NOTES** *This recipe came to me through my friend Joan Eckert, who says her family makes them at holiday time. As to the name,* mandel *means almond, but searches through Swedish dictionaries yield no information on* moussla. *Joan says, "that's just what we always called them." The best I can figure is that it is similar to the Swedish word for mousse, and once the cookies are topped with whipped cream and preserves, they are soft and mousse-like.*

❋ **LIFESPAN** *4 days unfilled at room temperature in airtight container*

Yield: *48 cookies*

❄ INGREDIENTS

Cookies:

2 cups all-purpose flour
¼ teaspoon salt
½ cup sliced blanched or natural almonds, chopped
1 cup (2 sticks) unsalted butter, softened
½ cup granulated sugar
1 teaspoon almond extract

1 teaspoon light or dark rum
1 large egg yolk

Topping:

¾ cup heavy cream
1 tablespoon granulated sugar
½ cup jam (preferably lingonberry, sour cherry, or other red-colored, tart jam)

❄ DIRECTIONS

1. Preheat oven to 375 degrees F. Coat four 12-cup mini-muffin tins with non-stick spray.

2. Whisk flour and salt together in a small bowl; stir in nuts.

3. In a large bowl with an electric mixer on medium-high speed, beat butter until creamy, about 2 minutes. Add sugar gradually, beating until light and fluffy, about 3 minutes; beat in almond extract and rum. Beat in egg yolk until combined. Add about one-third of flour mixture and mix on low speed. Gradually add remaining flour, mixing just until blended; dough will be very thick. Press 1 tablespoon of dough into each muffin well, leveling by pressing with a floured fingertip, then making a depression in the center of each one.

4. Bake until very light golden brown around edges, about 10 minutes. Cool in pans on racks for a couple of minutes, then carefully invert muffin pan, tap bottoms to release cookies, and transfer to racks to cool completely. (Can be stored at room temperature in an airtight container up to 4 days.)

5. Right before serving, in a small bowl with electric mixer on high speed, whip heavy cream and sugar together until stiff peaks form. Place whipped cream in pastry bag fitted with coupler and small closed-star tip (such as Ateco #18). Pipe a small ring of cream around edge of each cookie, leaving the depressed center open. Place a dollop of jam in the center of the whipped cream, down in depression. Serve within an hour.

Anise Cookies · *Bizcochitos*

❋ **TYPE** *Rolled cookie*　　❋ **HABITAT** *Mexico*

❋ **DESCRIPTION** *This crispy rolled sugar cookie is flavored with anise and lemon zest and topped with cinnamon sugar. The flavors come together in a gloriously harmonious way. I didn't think these would be kid-pleasers, but they are!*

❋ **FIELD NOTES** *These anise-flavored cookies are favored throughout the Southwest and New Mexico. Traditionally made with lard, which you may use, I have substituted vegetable shortening and added some butter for flavor. You can use a fleur-de-lis–shaped cookie cutter, which is popular, or any other shape you like.*

❋ **LIFESPAN** *2 weeks at room temperature in airtight container*

Yield: *seventy-two 2-inch cookies*

❆ **INGREDIENTS**

Cookies:
2⅓ cups all-purpose flour
½ teaspoon baking powder
¼ teaspoon salt
5 tablespoons unsalted butter, softened
¼ cup vegetable shortening
⅔ cup granulated sugar

2 teaspoons anise seeds, crushed
1 teaspoon finely grated lemon zest
1 large egg
1 large egg yolk

Topping:
1 tablespoon granulated sugar
1 teaspoon ground cinnamon

❆ **DIRECTIONS**

1. Whisk flour, baking powder, and salt together in a small bowl.

2. In a large bowl with an electric mixer on medium-high speed, beat butter and shortening together until creamy, about 2 minutes. Add sugar gradually, beating until light and fluffy, about 3 minutes; beat in anise seeds and zest. Add whole egg and egg yolk one at a time, beating well after each. Add about one-third of flour and mix on low speed. Gradually add remaining flour, mixing just until blended. Form dough into two very flat discs, cover with plastic wrap, and refrigerate until firm enough to roll out, at least 2 hours or overnight.

3. Preheat oven to 375 degrees F. Line 2 cookie sheets with parchment paper.

   To make topping, combine sugar and cinnamon in a small bowl.

4. Roll out one disc to ⅛-inch thickness on floured surface; you may need to flour rolling pin too. If dough is sticky, roll it between 2 pieces of floured parchment paper. Cut out cookies with shapes of choice and place 2 inches apart on cookie sheets. Sprinkle cookies with cinnamon sugar, taking care not to get too much on sheet.

5. Bake until light golden brown around the edges, about 10 minutes. Slide parchment onto racks to cool cookies completely.

Aunt Naomi's
Sacred Dog Biscuits

(Dedicated to bull terriers everywhere)

✳ **TYPE** *Rolled cookie* ✳ **HABITAT** *United States*

✳ **DESCRIPTION** *Yes, dog biscuits! For your pup, not you! Dog biscuits are actually very easy to make, and this recipe is not only delicious (so my canine testers tell me) but also nutritious, featuring lean chicken. You can find the bonemeal and either type of yeast in a health food store. If your doggie is sensitive to wheat, just use the rye flour.*

✳ **FIELD NOTES** *Beckett, our bull terrier, is the lucky recipient of these treats. The recipe was graciously given to me by Naomi Waynee and her MilleniuM bull terriers, Jessye, Tess, Six, and Angus.*

✳ **LIFESPAN** *1 month at room temperature in airtight container*

Yield: *forty 3-inch dog biscuits*

❊ INGREDIENTS

8 ounces boneless, skinless chicken breast
(about half a breast)
¾ cup chicken broth
1 large egg
1 tablespoon bonemeal

1 tablespoon brewer's or nutritional yeast
⅛ teaspoon garlic powder (not salt)
2½ cups whole wheat or rye flour
½ cup cornmeal

❊ DIRECTIONS

1. Place chicken breast in a small saucepan with enough water to cover. Bring to a boil over high heat. Reduce heat to medium-low and simmer until chicken is cooked through, about 10 minutes, turning it over at least once.

2. Preheat oven to 400 degrees F. Line 2 cookie sheets with parchment paper.

3. Measure out needed broth in 2-cup measuring cup, then add egg, bonemeal, yeast, and garlic powder, and stir to combine.

4. Place chicken in food processor and pulse until finely minced. With machine on, pour broth mixture through feed tube and process until evenly combined. Add flour and cornmeal and process until clumps appear and dough forms into a mass. Roll dough out to ⅜-inch thickness on lightly floured surface and cut out shapes of your choice; I use a dog-bone cutter. Place biscuits 1 inch apart on sheets. Prick all over with a fork.

5. Bake for 15 minutes, then reduce oven temperature to 350 degrees F and bake until completely dry and golden brown, about 1 hour. Slide parchment onto racks to cool cookies completely.

Benne Wafers

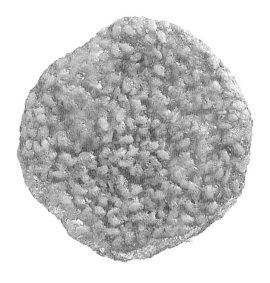

✳ **TYPE** *Drop cookies* ✳ **HABITAT** *United States*

✳ **DESCRIPTION** *These translucent, crunchy, brown sugary cookies are almost impossibly delicate looking, but are actually very easy to make. The batter comes together in one bowl and is stirred together by hand in less than 5 minutes. It features sesame seeds, which add a pretty look and subtle nutty taste. Make sure to drop them by the ¼ teaspoon because they really spread. These must be stored in an airtight container to retain their crispness. Don't be put off by the large yield; folks eat these by the half-dozen.*

✳ **FIELD NOTES** *This recipe was given to me by my friend Christopher Rivers, whose paternal grandmother passed down the recipe, written in her own hand; he and his mom have made adjustments over the years. Sesame seeds are called "benne" seeds in the South Carolina low country (the coastal area around Charleston). They were brought over by slaves from West Africa and, at least according to local tradition, were thought by them to bring good luck, hence their use in cooking.*

✳ **LIFESPAN** *2 weeks at room temperature in airtight container*

Yield: *120 cookies*

❋ INGREDIENTS

1 tablespoon unsalted butter, softened
1 cup firmly packed light brown sugar
1 large egg
½ cup white sesame seeds

2 tablespoons all-purpose flour
½ teaspoon vanilla extract
¼ teaspoon salt

❋ DIRECTIONS

1. Preheat oven to 350 degrees F. Line 2 cookie sheets with parchment paper and coat lightly with nonstick spray.

2. Beat the butter in a medium-size bowl with a wooden spoon. Add brown sugar, and stir vigorously to combine. Beat in egg until combined. Add sesame seeds, flour, vanilla, and salt, and stir until combined. Drop onto cookie sheets by ¼ teaspoonfuls at least 2 inches apart.

3. Bake until medium golden brown, about 7 minutes. They will have spread to about 1½ inches in diameter and have become crisp around the edges, although the golden brown color will be uniform over the whole cookie. They will firm up upon cooling, however, and will still be soft in the middle even when fully cooked. Place sheets on racks and let cookies cool.

Bow Ties ❄ *Chrusti*

❄ **TYPE** *Fried cookie*   ❄ **HABITAT** *Poland*

❄ **DESCRIPTION** *These deep-fried cookies, tied in a knot shape, are given a snowy dusting of confectioners' sugar as they cool. A deep-fat fryer makes these easier to make, but you can use a deep pot and a thermometer. These are best eaten soon after frying.*

❄ **FIELD NOTES** *Many countries have deep-fried cookies such as these, sometimes called love knots. This recipe was given to me by Angie Czajkowski, who says these are always made during the holidays. Pigs were often slaughtered for the holiday meal, which meant there would be plenty of fat available for these deep-fried treats.*

❄ **LIFESPAN** *3 days at room temperature in airtight container*

Yield: *75 cookies*

❄ INGREDIENTS

5 large eggs
1 tablespoon light or dark rum
½ teaspoon vanilla extract
3¼ cups all-purpose flour
½ cup granulated sugar

Pinch of salt
2 tablespoons (¼ stick) unsalted butter, softened
Vegetable oil or shortening for frying
Confectioners' sugar

❄ DIRECTIONS

1. In a large bowl with an electric mixer on high speed, beat eggs until thick and creamy. Beat in rum and vanilla. Wash and dry beaters of mixer.

2. In another large bowl, combine flour, granulated sugar, and salt. Add butter and beat on medium speed until mixture has an even crumb. Add wet mixture to dry, beating on medium-low speed until a soft but not sticky dough forms. Run mixer for a minute or two to knead dough.

3. Heat 2 inches of oil or shortening (or a blend) in a deep-fat fryer or deep, heavy pot to 375 degrees F.

4. Roll dough out to ⅛-inch thickness on lightly floured surface. Cut a grid, using a sharp knife or a pizza cutter, making 1½ x 5-inch rectangles. Make a 1-inch slit lengthwise in the center of each rectangle. Pull one end of strip through the slit, forming a loose knot for each cookie. Stretch each piece out gently to form bow-tie shapes.

5. Add a few knots to the hot fat at a time and fry for about 1 minute, then flip over using tongs and fry until light golden brown on all sides, about 1 minute more. Do not crowd; the knots need room to move around. Remove using slotted spoon and drain on paper towels. Repeat with remaining knots.

6. While cookies are still warm, place on a rimmed cookie sheet or in a large bowl, sift confectioners' sugar over them, and gently toss to coat heavily. I like these best within a few hours of frying.

Brandy Snaps

❋ **TYPE** *Drop cookie*   ❋ **HABITAT** *England*

❋ **DESCRIPTION** *These lacy, gingery cookies are rolled around a wooden spoon handle while warm. They can be served as is, or filled with brandy-flavored whipped cream. The key with these cookies is to bake just a few at a time so that you can roll them while they are still warm—and bake on a dry day. Humidity wreaks havoc with their crisp texture.*

❋ **FIELD NOTES** *These classic British cookies do require a special ingredient called golden syrup, which can be ordered from King Arthur Flour The Baker's Catalogue (see Resources). In a pinch, substitute light corn syrup.*

❋ **LIFESPAN** *2 weeks unfilled at room temperature in airtight container*

Yield: *40 cookies*

❄ INGREDIENTS

Cookies:
¾ cup all-purpose flour
1 teaspoon ground ginger
Pinch of salt
½ cup (1 stick) unsalted butter
⅔ cup golden syrup or light corn syrup
½ cup granulated sugar
1 tablespoon brandy

Filling (optional):
1½ cups heavy cream
1 tablespoon plus 2 teaspoons granulated sugar
1 teaspoon brandy

❄ DIRECTIONS

1. Preheat oven to 350 degrees F. Line 2 cookie sheets with parchment paper.

2. Whisk flour, ginger, and salt together in a small bowl.

3. Combine butter, syrup, and sugar in a medium saucepan over medium heat. Bring to a boil, let boil 30 seconds, remove from heat, and slowly whisk in brandy. Then whisk in flour mixture until batter is smooth. Drop batter by generously rounded teaspoon several inches apart on cookie sheets, allowing them plenty of space to spread, a maximum of 5 per sheet. (More will fit, but they will cool too quickly for you to roll them while still warm.)

4. Bake until lacy and evenly golden brown, about 8 minutes. Remove from oven and place sheet on rack to cool until cookies are firm enough to lift with a metal spatula or your fingers, but still flexible, about 1 minute. Working quickly, one at a time, wrap a cookie, top lacy side facing outward, around an oiled wooden spoon handle about ⅓ inch in diameter. Press gently on the seam, then slide cookie off handle and place on rack to cool completely. If cookies become too firm to roll, simply return cookie sheet to oven for a moment or two.

5. Right before serving, if desired, whip heavy cream, sugar, and brandy in a large bowl with an electric mixer on high speed until medium stiff peaks form. Scrape into pastry bag fitted with coupler and small star tip (such as Ateco #18) and pipe cream into both ends of rolled cookies; serve immediately.

GOOD COOKIE TIP

If you would like to forgo the rolling technique, simple leave the cookies flat and serve as is. They are crispy, sweet, and delicious any which way. Another variation is to use Grand Marnier, which is an orange brandy, in both the cookie and whipped cream.

Candy Cane Cookies

✳ **TYPE** *Shaped cookie*   ✳ **HABITAT** *United States*

✳ **DESCRIPTION** *These decorative cookies are made by twisting a pale red dough and a white dough together and forming small candy cane shapes. They also pack the punch of peppermint, both from extract and crushed candy canes.*

✳ **FIELD NOTES** *Americans seem to have a fascination with crafty cookies, and this has got to be the ultimate example of a Christmas cookie that requires a little handiwork; it's got the flavors, colors, and shape of Christmas all in one cookie. Versions of these cookies seem to find their way into women's magazines every holiday season and crop up on cookie platters from coast to coast.*

✳ **LIFESPAN** *2 weeks at room temperature in airtight container; make sure to store separately from any other cookie or they will all end up tasting like peppermint*

Yield: *100 cookies*

❄ INGREDIENTS

3½ cups all-purpose flour
¼ teaspoon salt
1 cup (2 sticks) unsalted butter, softened
¾ cup granulated sugar
1 teaspoon vanilla extract
1 large egg

2 tablespoons finely crushed red-and-
white peppermint candy (from candy
canes or drops)
½ teaspoon peppermint extract
12 drops red liquid food coloring

❄ DIRECTIONS

1. Whisk flour and salt together in a small bowl.

2. In a large bowl with an electric mixer on medium-high speed, beat butter until creamy, about 2 minutes. Add sugar gradually, beating until light and fluffy, about 3 minutes. Beat in vanilla and egg. Add about one-third of flour and mix on low speed. Gradually add remaining flour, mixing just until blended. Remove half of dough and cover with plastic wrap. Add crushed candy, extract, and food coloring to dough remaining in bowl and beat on low speed until well blended. Cover dough with plastic wrap as well and refrigerate both until firm enough to roll out, at least 2 hours or overnight.

3. Preheat oven to 350 degrees F. Line 2 cookie sheets with parchment paper.

4. Separately roll ½ teaspoon of dough of each color on a lightly floured surface into a ¼-inch-wide, 5-inch-long rope. Twist them together, place 2 inches apart on cookie sheets, and shape into a small candy cane by curving about a quarter of the length of twisted rope into a hook shape.

5. Bake until just beginning to turn light golden brown around edges, about 12 minutes. Place pan on rack to cool.

GOOD COOKIE TIP

To crush candy canes, pulverize in food processor or, alternatively, place unwrapped candy canes or drops in a zipper-lock plastic bag and roll a rolling pin back and forth over bag until candies are finely and evenly crushed.

Cardamom Wafers · *Krumkake*

❄ **TYPE** *Pressed and filled*   ❄ **HABITAT** *Scandinavia*

❄ **DESCRIPTION** *These are very thin, crispy wafer-like cookies, formed into a cone, which you can then fill with sweetened whipped cream. You need a* krumkake *maker; they come in metal models that you use on your stove top, and there are nonstick electric models, which I highly recommend. I use a nonstick VillaWare model, and this recipe's batter and size of cookie is based upon using it; most* krumkake *makers will come with a wooden device to help you roll the cookie.*

❄ **FIELD NOTES** *These are very similar to Italian* pizzelle *(page 118) in that a fairly simple batter is made and most of the impact comes from the form they take, which is quite decorative. Cardamom is a frequently used spice in Scandinavia, and it gives these cookies a fragrant, elusive flavor. By the way, the cookie is pronounced "KROOM-kah-kah."*

❄ **LIFESPAN** *1 week unfilled at room temperature in airtight container*

Yield: *30* krumkake

❄ INGREDIENTS

Cookies:
1⅔ cups cake flour
4 large eggs
1 cup granulated sugar
½ cup (1 stick) unsalted butter, melted
    and cooled

½ teaspoon ground cardamom
½ teaspoon vanilla extract

Filling:
1 cup heavy cream
1 tablespoon granulated sugar

❄ DIRECTIONS

1. Whisk flour in a small bowl.

2. Whisk eggs and sugar together in a medium bowl until blended and smooth, about 1 minute. Whisk in melted butter until combined; whisk in cardamom and vanilla. Gradually add flour, whisking or stirring until blended.

3. Preheat *krumkake* maker according to manufacturer's instructions. Drop by generously rounded teaspoon per *krumkake* and cook for less than a minute, until just starting to turn golden around edges, but still soft. Remove carefully with fingertips or edge of an icing spatula and immediately roll around wooden cone, decorative side facing out. Gently press around cone to help cookie form its shape, and allow to sit on cone for 30 seconds. Cookie will begin to cool and take shape; then place directly on rack to cool completely.

4. To make filling, in a medium bowl with an electric mixer on high speed, whip heavy cream and sugar together until soft peaks form. Scrape mixture into pastry bag fitted with large star tip (such as Ateco #844) and pipe whipped cream into cavity of each cookie. Serve immediately.

GOOD COOKIE TIP

As with pizzelle makers, krumkake makers will vary in design, size, and the way they work. Just as when you make waffles, you have to get the hang of your particular machine in terms of amount of batter and length of cooking time. Just use the visual cues to help you along.

Cherry Orange Florentines

❄ **TYPE** *Drop cookie*   ❄ **HABITAT** *Italy*

❄ **DESCRIPTION** *These might possibly be the most addictive, scrumptious cookies I have ever tasted. Be prepared to be unable to resist the chewy and crunchy combination of caramel, chocolate, orange, cherries, and almonds.*

❄ **FIELD NOTES** *One important technique to know: it is vital to have the dried cherries, candied orange peel, and sliced almonds evenly and finely chopped. Every piece should be between ⅛ and ¼ inch. There will be some variation, which is okay, but try to get the pieces as equal as possible. If you have a candy thermometer, this recipe will be easier, but I have given you directions to follow if you don't. Also, these really spread, so space them as suggested.*

❄ **LIFESPAN** *1 week refrigerated in airtight container in single layers separated by waxed paper*

Yield: *36 cookies*

❄ INGREDIENTS

6 tablespoons (¾ stick) unsalted butter
⅔ cup granulated sugar
⅓ cup heavy cream
3 tablespoons honey
1 cup sliced natural almonds, finely chopped

⅓ cup dried cherries, finely chopped
⅓ cup minced candied orange peel
¼ cup all-purpose flour
6 ounces semisweet or bittersweet chocolate, finely chopped

❄ DIRECTIONS

1. Preheat oven to 350 degrees F. Line 2 cookie sheets with parchment paper.

2. Place butter, sugar, heavy cream, and honey in a medium saucepan and bring to a boil. Swirl pan around a few times to blend ingredients. Reduce heat until mixture is at a low boil and cook to 230 degrees F on a candy thermometer (if you dip a spoon into the mixture and dribble it in a glass of cold water, it will spin a thread). Stir almonds, cherries, candied peel, and flour into cream mixture with a wooden spoon until evenly combined. Scrape mixture into a bowl (it will cool more quickly) and allow to cool to room temperature. Stir occasionally to release heat; mixture will thicken.

3. Drop by generously rounded teaspoon 4 inches apart on cookie sheets. The rounder your "drops," the rounder, and more attractive, your baked cookies will be.

4. Bake until an even golden brown (absolutely remember to shift pans front to back halfway through), about 12 minutes. Cookies will bubble and spread and possibly lose their round shape. Place pans on rack. If the cookies are misshapen, immediately coax them into a round shape by pushing in stray edges with side of an offset spatula (or butter knife) dipped in hot water. Slide parchment onto racks to cool cookies completely.

5. Meanwhile, temper chocolate as directed on page 10. Carefully remove cooled cookies from sheet with spatula or your fingers. Using a small offset spatula, spread chocolate over bottoms of cookies. Make a wavy pattern with a decorator's comb or fork, if desired. Place cookies, chocolate side up, back on sheet. Place in refrigerator until chocolate is set.

Chocolate Bourbon Balls

❋ **TYPE** *Shaped confection*   ❋ **HABITAT** *United States*

❋ **DESCRIPTION** *This no-bake confection always seems to find its way into cookie collections since it is so easy to prepare and makes a great holiday treat or gift. A combination of crushed cookie crumbs, ground nuts, sugar, chocolate, and bourbon, with a little corn syrup to help hold them together, they have a pleasantly chewy texture. These are best if aged at least overnight, and even better after a few days. Some say they hit their peak after a month, so plan accordingly.*

❋ **FIELD NOTES** *There are many versions of bourbon-flavored balls featuring cookie crumbs, some going back to the 1930s. Older versions often use cocoa as the chocolate component. This recipe, with melted chocolate, is a newer, and richer, incarnation. These are particularly popular in the Southeast, where bourbon is a favored beverage and flavoring. This version came to me courtesy of Christina Trivero and her family.*

❋ **RELATED SPECIES** Chocolate Rum Balls: *Substitute dark rum for bourbon;* Tipsy Chocolate Orange Rum Balls: *Substitute Grand Marnier for bourbon;* Toasted Mocha Balls: *Substitute Kahlua for bourbon.*

❋ **LIFESPAN** *1½ months at room temperature in airtight container*

Yield: *50 balls*

❋ INGREDIENTS

2½ cups vanilla wafer crumbs (Nilla
Wafers or similar cookie)
½ cup confectioners' sugar, sifted
1 cup pecan halves, finely ground in food
processor

6 ounces semisweet or bittersweet
chocolate, broken into pieces
½ cup bourbon
3 tablespoons light corn syrup
Granulated sugar

❋ DIRECTIONS

1. Place cookie crumbs, confectioners' sugar, and ground pecans in a large bowl and stir to combine.

2. Melt the chocolate in microwave or in top of double boiler over simmering water. Stir in bourbon and corn syrup. Add chocolate mixture to dry mixture and stir well to combine. Let sit for 30 minutes. Place some granulated sugar in a small bowl.

3. Roll mixture between your palms into 1-inch balls, then roll in sugar to coat evenly. Place balls in airtight container, separating layers with aluminum foil or waxed paper, and allow flavors to develop by sitting at room temperature at least overnight. You may first place them in small fluted paper cups, if desired.

Chocolate Chipzels

❋ **TYPE** *Drop cookie*   ❋ **HABITAT** *United States*

❋ **DESCRIPTION** *I am not a junk-food junkie, but these candies can convert even the likes of me. They come together in a flash, and the combination of salty, crunchy potato chips and pretzels with deep, dark chocolate is irresistible. If you like coconut, try that variation, too.*

❋ **FIELD NOTES** *This recipe takes advantage of convenience foods, in this case pretzels and potato chips. Many upscale candy emporiums sell chocolate-dipped pretzels and chocolate-dipped potato chips, and that is where I got my inspiration.*

❋ **LIFESPAN** *1 month refrigerated in airtight container in single layers separated by waxed paper*

Yield: *30 chipzels*

❋ INGREDIENTS

I pound semisweet chocolate, broken into pieces

1½ cups crushed pretzels (such as Rold Gold Classic Style Tiny Twists)

1½ cups crushed ridged potato chips

I cup plus 2 tablespoons sweetened flaked coconut (optional)

❋ DIRECTIONS

1. Line 2 cookie sheets with parchment paper and coat with nonstick spray.

2. Melt chocolate either in microwave or in top of double boiler over simmering water; stir until smooth. Gently fold in 1¼ cups each crushed pretzels and potato chips until combined. Fold in 1 cup coconut, if using.

3. Drop by generously rounded tablespoon about 1 inch apart on cookie sheets. Take remaining ¼ cup each pretzels and potato chips (and 2 tablespoons coconut, if using) and place pieces here and there on top of mounds to indicate what is folded inside the chocolate and give a decorative look. Refrigerate until completely firm, about 1 hour.

Chocolate-Dipped Almond Drops

❄ **TYPE** *Shaped cookie*   ❄ **HABITAT** *United States*

❄ **DESCRIPTION** *These chewy, nutty cookies are very simple to make and look very fancy. To get the best flavor and texture, used canned almond paste, not the kind that comes in a tube.*

❄ **FIELD NOTES** *Any cookie containing almond paste has European roots, but these cookies, often made very large and in a horseshoe shape, are popular in American bakeries and delicatessens. I chose to make these small and round, as they are more versatile in their diminutive state during the holidays. If you would like to make them larger, roll about 2 tablespoons of dough into a very thin log, roll in almonds, and shape into a* U *on the prepared sheet. After cooling, dip both ends in melted chocolate.*

❄ **LIFESPAN** *3 days at room temperature in airtight container*

Yield: *30 cookies*

❄ INGREDIENTS

½ pound canned almond paste
¾ cup plus 1 tablespoon granulated sugar
2 large egg whites

1 cup sliced natural almonds
8 ounces bittersweet or semisweet
chocolate, broken into pieces

❄ DIRECTIONS

1. Preheat oven to 350 degrees F. Line 2 cookie sheets with parchment paper.

2. Place almond paste and sugar in a large bowl and beat with an electric mixer on medium-high speed until creamy, about 2 minutes. Add egg whites and beat on medium speed until smooth, about 2 minutes.

3. Place almonds in a shallow dish, such as a pie plate. Roll pieces of dough between your palms into 1-inch balls. Roll around in almonds to coat com-pletely and place 2 inches apart on cookie sheets.

4. Bake until light golden brown around edges, puffed, and pale gold on top, about 15 minutes. Slide parchment onto racks to cool cookies completely.

5. Temper chocolate as directed on page 10. Dip cooled cookies sideways halfway into chocolate; allow excess chocolate to drip back into pot. Place cookies back on sheet and place in refrigerator until chocolate is set.

Cinnamon Ornaments

❄ **TYPE** *Rolled cookie*   ❄ **HABITAT** *United States*

❄ **DESCRIPTION** *Believe it or not, if you stir enough cinnamon into applesauce, you can create a dough that can be rolled out and cut into shapes. After drying, they make wonderfully fragrant ornaments for hanging on your tree. Do not eat these; they are for decoration only. P.S.: Don't bother making homemade applesauce—the jarred kind is just fine.*

❄ **FIELD NOTES** *I had seen these ornaments at craft fairs for years, and when someone told me how they were made, I didn't believe it. Then, when I was working on this book, I found literally dozens of versions, all essentially the same, on the Internet. I have no idea where they originated. If you know, e-mail me and fill me in!*

❄ **LIFESPAN** *Forever*

Yield: *about thirty 2- to 3-inch ornaments*

❄ INGREDIENTS

Cookies:

2 cups jarred no-sugar-added applesauce
2¼ cups ground cinnamon, plus more for
  rolling out
¼ cup ground ginger

Decoration:

10 yards ⅛-inch fabric ribbon, cut into
  12-inch lengths

❄ DIRECTIONS

1. Have ready 2 cookie sheets.

2. Combine applesauce, cinnamon, and
   ginger in a large bowl until spices are
   completely incorporated and mixture is
   stiff enough to roll out. Add more cinnamon if necessary.

3. Roll dough out to ¼-inch thickness on
   surface lightly sprinkled with cinnamon. Cut out shapes of your choice;
   insert end of a chopstick in top of each
   ornament and swirl around until a
   hole is formed. You can also use a
   drinking straw. Transfer to

cookie sheets and allow to dry 12
hours or overnight. Gently turn over,
dry for 12 more hours, and repeat until
completely hard and dry. Drying
process might take a few days.

4. Thread ribbon through hole and knot
   about 1 inch from the ends. They are
   now ready to hang.

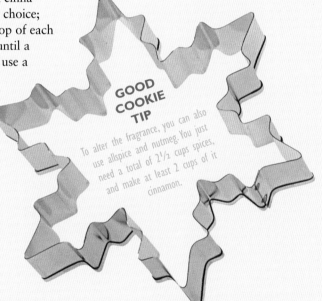

GOOD COOKIE TIP

To alter the fragrance, you can also use allspice and nutmeg. You just need a total of 2½ cups spices, and make at least 2 cups of it cinnamon.

Cinnamon Stars · *Zimtsterne*

❄ **TYPE** *Rolled cookie*   ❄ **HABITAT** *Germany*

❄ **DESCRIPTION** *These are unlike any other cookie I have ever read about, made, or eaten—and I absolutely love them! They begin with a meringue flavored with lemon zest and cinnamon and packed with ground almonds. The resulting meringue is so thick you can roll it out. The dough is delicate, but the results are worth it. To literally gild the lily, consider the optional edible gold decoration; while not traditional, it is a knockout.*

❄ **FIELD NOTES** *While specifics of the history of Zimtsterne remain elusive, they have been and are still very popular in German-speaking countries.*

❄ **LIFESPAN** *2 weeks at room temperature in airtight container*

Yield: *sixty 1½-inch stars*

❄ **INGREDIENTS**

Cookies:
2 cups blanched whole almonds
2 cups confectioners' sugar, sifted, plus
  more for rolling out
2 large egg whites
1½ teaspoons finely grated lemon zest
1 teaspoon ground cinnamon

Decoration (optional):
Edible gold powder
Vodka
Soft artist's brush

❄ **DIRECTIONS**

1. Combine almonds and ½ cup confectioners' sugar in food processor and process until nuts are very finely ground.

2. In a large, clean, grease-free bowl with an electric mixer on high speed, whip egg whites until soft peaks form. Gradually add remaining 1½ cups confectioners' sugar, whipping until thick and creamy. Remove ¼ cup meringue and set aside.

3. Fold ground almond mixture, lemon zest, and cinnamon into larger portion of meringue. Mixture will be stiff. Allow to sit for 30 minutes at room temperature.

   Preheat oven to 275 degrees F. Line 2 cookie sheets with parchment paper.

4. Roll dough out to ¼-inch thickness on surface sprinkled with confectioners' sugar. Cut out small stars (about 1½ inches across) and place at least 2 inches apart on cookie sheets. Brush with reserved meringue, taking care to cover entire surface evenly and not allow any meringue to drip down sides.

5. Bake until bottoms are light golden brown, about 20 minutes; meringue should remain white and be very dry. Slide parchment onto racks to cool cookies completely.

6. To decorate, if desired, place a small amount of gold powder in a small bowl and add vodka, a few drops at a time, until a thick paint consistency is reached. Paint the top edges of star with gold paint or paint entire meringue surface. Allow to dry.

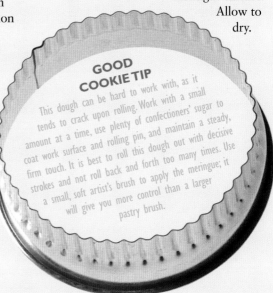

GOOD COOKIE TIP

This dough can be hard to work with, as it tends to crack upon rolling. Work with a small amount at a time, use plenty of confectioners' sugar to coat work surface and rolling pin, and maintain a steady, firm touch. It is best to roll this dough out with decisive strokes and not roll back and forth too many times. Use a small, soft artist's brush to apply the meringue; it will give you more control than a larger pastry brush.

Coconut Snowballs

❄ **TYPE** *Drop cookie*   ❄ **HABITAT** *United States*

❄ **DESCRIPTION** *These are somewhat crunchy on the outside and tender in the middle, but they are coconut through and through—coconut lovers only need apply.*

❄ **FIELD NOTES** *You need two kinds of coconut for this cookie. The unsweetened coconut, which you can usually find in bulk sections in natural foods stores, has a very fine texture and keeps the cookie from being too sweet. The sweetened flaked coconut adds a chewy texture and sweetness.*

❄ **RELATED SPECIES** Chocolate Coconut Snowballs: *Temper 8 ounces bittersweet or semisweet chocolate (page 10) and dip bottoms of cookies in it, coming up about ½ inch. Allow excess chocolate to drip back into pot of chocolate. Place chocolate side up (they'll kind of be on their sides) on cookie sheet and refrigerate until chocolate hardens. These are best eaten the day they are made.*

❄ **LIFESPAN** *4 days at room temperature in airtight container*

Yield: *15 snowballs*

❄ INGREDIENTS

4 large egg whites
¾ cup granulated sugar
1 teaspoon vanilla extract

1½ cups unsweetened grated coconut
(5 ounces)
1½ cups sweetened flaked coconut
(4 ounces)

❄ DIRECTIONS

1. Preheat oven to 375 degrees F. Line 2 cookie sheets with parchment paper; coat lightly with nonstick spray.

2. Whisk together egg whites, sugar, and vanilla in top of a double boiler (not over hot water yet) until combined. Add both types of coconut and fold in until coconut is completely coated with the egg-white mixture. Place over simmering water with the water just touching the bottom. Stir mixture constantly; the sugar will dissolve and mixture become glossy and hot to the touch in about 3 minutes. Drop 2 tablespoon-size mounds 1½ inches apart on cookie sheets. Cookies should be round and very three-dimensional; do not flatten. If needed, coax into a neat shape with fingers by pressing any stray shreds around edges into cookie mound.

3. Bake until edges and some of coconut shreds turn light golden brown, about 13 minutes. Slide parchment onto racks to cool cookies completely before peeling off paper.

Cookies in a Jar

✳ **TYPE** *Drop cookie*   ✳ **HABITAT** *United States*

✳ **DESCRIPTION** *This recipe is not for cookies per se, but for carefully and decoratively arranged ingredients. You layer colorful and distinct cookie ingredients in a jar, attach a note card, and give it as a gift—the gift of almost-instant cookies. This version, of which there are many, features chocolate chips and multicolored candy-covered morsels. Success depends on making the layers of ingredients even and packing down each one as you go, or they won't fit in the jar. You'll need a 1-quart, widemouthed canning jar with a lid for this.*

✳ **FIELD NOTES** *My son's school made these as a fundraiser for their sixth-grade class trip, and this is where I became familiar with them. I have seen many recipes for "cookies in a jar," including oatmeal-raisin and brownie versions, both in magazine advertisements and on the Internet. I have no idea where the concept originated, but it is brilliant!*

Yield: *1 jar, 30 cookies*

❄ INGREDIENTS

Cookies:
1¾ cups all-purpose flour
1 teaspoon baking soda
¼ teaspoon salt
¾ cup firmly packed light brown sugar
½ cup granulated sugar
¼ cup Dutch-processed unsweetened cocoa powder, sifted
½ cup finely chopped walnuts

½ cup semisweet chocolate chips
½ cup candy-coated chocolate candies (such as M&Ms)

Decoration:
Note card
Hole-punch
8-inch square of decorative fabric
Rubber band
24 inches of ½-inch ribbon

❄ DIRECTIONS

1. Whisk flour, baking soda, and salt together in a small bowl.

2. Make sure jar is clean and completely dry. Pour flour mixture into jar and pack down firmly into an even layer using the bottom of a small ladle or rubber spatula. Pour brown sugar into jar and tap down firmly (tapping down the brown sugar will help pack the flour layer beneath it). Follow with an even layer of granulated sugar, then a layer of cocoa powder, again packing down as you go. Wipe down sides of jar after cocoa is added, as some of it might cling. Add layer of nuts, followed by a layer of chocolate chips, then the candies, and tap down those ingredients. Screw top into place.

3. Make a hole in the corner of the notecard with hole-punch. Write the following directions on card, along with any sentiments you might have for the receiver:

Candy Cookies in a Jar
Preheat oven to 350 degrees F and line two cookie sheets with parchment paper. Melt 1½ sticks unsalted butter on stove or in large bowl in microwave; allow to cool. Whisk in 1 large egg and 1 teaspoon vanilla extract. Add contents of jar and stir until well combined; you might need to use your hands. Drop by generously rounded tablespoon 2 inches apart on prepared cookie sheets and press to flatten. Bake until tops are cracked and dry; they will be soft on top and in the middle, about 12 minutes. Cookies will firm up upon cooling. Slide parchment onto racks to cool cookies completely. (Can be stored at room temperature in an airtight container up to 1 week.) Enjoy, and Happy Baking!

4. Center fabric over top of jar and slip on rubber band to hold it in place just under lid. Place ribbon over rubber band and tie ribbon by making the first step of tying a bow. Slip ribbon through hole in note card, then tie a bow.

Cranberry Snowdrift Bars

❄ **TYPE** *Bar cookie*   ❄ **HABITAT** *United States*

❄ **DESCRIPTION** *These pretty bars start with a shortbread crust topped with a tart cranberry filling. Then the bars are embellished with a thick, snowy white layer of sweet meringue, swirled and peaked to resemble snowdrifts.*

❄ **FIELD NOTES** *In American cookbooks, particularly ones from the mid-twentieth century, there are many recipes for raspberry bars topped with a meringue. That is where I got the idea for this cranberry version.*

❄ **LIFESPAN** *2 days at room temperature in airtight container*

Yield: *20 bars*

❄ INGREDIENTS

Crust:
1 ¼ cups all-purpose flour
Pinch of salt
½ cup (1 stick) unsalted butter, softened
¼ cup granulated sugar
¼ teaspoon vanilla extract

Filling and topping:
1 cup whole-berry cranberry sauce, not
   jellied (such as Ocean Spray Whole-
   Berry Cranberry Sauce)
2 large egg whites
⅛ teaspoon cream of tartar
½ cup granulated sugar
¼ teaspoon vanilla extract

❄ DIRECTIONS

1. Coat an 8-inch square baking pan with nonstick spray.

2. Whisk flour and salt together in a small bowl.

3. In a large bowl with an electric mixer on medium-high speed, beat butter until creamy, about 3 minutes. Add sugar gradually, beating on high speed until light and fluffy. This may take as long as 8 minutes. Do not rush; mixture should be almost white in color. Beat in vanilla. Add about one-third of flour and mix on low speed. Gradually add remaining flour, mixing just until blended. Pat crust in an even layer in baking pan. Refrigerate at least 30 minutes or overnight. Wash and dry beaters of mixer.

4. Preheat oven to 350 degrees F. Bake crust until completely dry to touch and a pale golden brown, about 40 minutes. The edges will be a bit darker. Place pan on rack to cool 5 minutes, then spread cranberry sauce evenly over crust using a small offset spatula or back of a spoon.

5. To make topping, whip egg whites until foamy in a medium clean, grease-free bowl with mixer on high speed. Add cream of tartar and whip until soft peaks form. Add sugar gradually, whipping until stiff but not dry peaks form. Beat in vanilla. Spread meringue evenly over cranberry layer. Use back of a teaspoon to make peaks and swirls in meringue.

6. Bake until meringue is a light golden brown, about 25 minutes. Place pan on rack to cool. Cut into 20 bars (4 x 5).

GOOD COOKIE TIP

For convenience, I have used canned cranberry sauce, but feel free to use your own. Just make sure it is thick and not at all watery.

Cream Cheese Almond Poinsettia Drops

※ **TYPE** *Shaped cookie*   ※ **HABITAT** *United States*

※ **DESCRIPTION** *This recipe is not only pretty, with slivered candied cherries and a white chocolate chip forming a flower on top of the cookies, but it is also tender and rich, thanks to the cream cheese in the batter. You might be able to find the candied cherry halves in your supermarket, but an excellent-quality candied cherry can be ordered from King Arthur Flour The Baker's Catalogue (see Resources).*

※ **FIELD NOTES** *I have seen many recipes for cookies with a poinsettia theme in American cookbooks; we Americans seem to love to play with our food in a crafty way, and this cookie is no exception. Some forgo flavor for appearance, but these taste as great as they look.*

※ **LIFESPAN** *1 week at room temperature in airtight container*

Yield: *85 cookies*

❄ INGREDIENTS

Cookies:
2 ½ cups all-purpose flour
I cup (2 sticks) unsalted butter, softened
One 3-ounce package cream cheese,
  softened
I cup granulated sugar
I teaspoon almond extract
I large egg yolk

Topping:
½ cup blanched whole almonds, toasted
  (page 11) and finely chopped
½ cup granulated sugar
I large egg white
85 candied cherry halves, sliced into slivers
85 white chocolate chips

❄ DIRECTIONS

1. Whisk flour in a small bowl.

2. In a large bowl with an electric mixer on medium-high speed, beat butter and cream cheese together until creamy, about 2 minutes. Add sugar gradually, beating until light and fluffy, about 3 minutes; beat in almond extract. Beat in egg yolk. Add about one-third of flour and mix on low speed. Gradually add remaining flour, mixing just until blended. Scrape dough onto a large piece of plastic wrap. Use wrap to help shape into a large, flat disc, then cover completely with wrap. Refrigerate until firm enough to roll into balls, at least 1 hour or overnight.

3. Preheat oven to 325 degrees F. Line 2 rimmed cookie sheets with parchment paper. Toss chopped nuts and sugar together in a small bowl. Whisk egg white until frothy.

4. Roll dough between your palms into 1-inch balls. Dip "top" of balls into egg white, then into nut-sugar mixture. Place 2 inches apart on cookie sheets, nut side up, and gently press to slightly flatten. Place 5 cherry slivers, outside of cherry skin facing up, in radiating ring on top of each cookie to form a petal

pattern—like a poinsettia! Then place a single chocolate chip upside down or right side up, depending on effect you like, in center of cookie. Press it in to adhere.

5. Bake until light golden brown around edges, about 22 minutes. Slide parchment onto racks to cool cookies completely.

GOOD COOKIE TIP

If you are short on time, forgo the slivering of the candied cherries and just press a cherry half, rounded side up, into the top of each cookie. Bury the chocolate chip inside the cherry half, if you like, for a surprise.

Date Chews

✻ **TYPE** *Bar cookie*   ✻ **HABITAT** *United States*

✻ **DESCRIPTION** *These chewy date cookies are baked in a pan, cut like bars, and then rolled in confectioners' sugar to give them a pleasant and unusual knobby shape. These have a cracked, crunchy top, are packed full of dates and walnuts, and keep extremely well, which is great during the holidays. What is also Christmasy about them is that the first time I made them as a child was during the holiday season when I was looking through cookbooks for a cookie that was different from all the others—this fits the bill.*

✻ **FIELD NOTES** *I have seen many recipes that are similar in that they have an abundance of dates, nuts, eggs, and sugar but very little flour. For some reason, they are sometimes called Chinese chews, perhaps because dates are associated with that area of the world. Chinese dates, or jujubes, are a fruit with many similarities to the dates that we know.*

✻ **LIFESPAN** *3 weeks at room temperature in airtight container*

Yield: *36 cookies*

❄ INGREDIENTS

1 cup packed pitted dates	3 large eggs
3 tablespoons all-purpose flour	1 cup granulated sugar
1 cup walnut halves	1 teaspoon vanilla extract
½ teaspoon baking powder	1 cup confectioners' sugar, sifted
¼ teaspoon salt	

❄ DIRECTIONS

1. Preheat oven to 325 degrees F. Coat a 9-inch square baking pan with nonstick spray.

2. Place dates and flour in food processor, pulse to combine, then process until dates are finely chopped. Scrape mixture into a large bowl. Add nuts to food processor and pulse until finely chopped. Add date-flour mixture back to processor along with baking powder and salt and quickly pulse to break up sticky dates and create a uniform mixture.

3. In a large bowl with an electric mixer on high speed, beat eggs, granulated sugar, and vanilla together until light and creamy, about 2 minutes. Add about one-third of date-flour mixture and mix on low speed. Gradually add remaining date-flour mixture, mixing just until blended. Scrape into baking pan, spreading evenly.

4. Bake until an even light golden brown all over, about 40 minutes; toothpick inserted in center should come out clean. Place pan on rack to cool for 5 minutes. Cut into 36 bars (6 x 6) while still warm. Place confectioners' sugar in a small bowl. Roll each square in it to coat completely while still warm, shaping the squares into rough barrel shapes as you go. Each cookie will be a unique, rustic shape. Place each cookie on rack to cool completely.

Dutch Windmill Cookies
Speculaas

❅ **TYPE** *Molded cookie*   ❅ **HABITAT** *Holland*

❅ **DESCRIPTION** *These pale brown, lightly spiced cookies are simply delicious, and the dough is very easy to roll out. You can use special* speculaas *molds or treat them like any rolled cookie and use cookie cutters. Either way, a windmill shape is traditional.*

❅ **FIELD NOTES** *The name of this cookie derives from the word for "mirror."* Speculaas *molds often depict windmills, animals, or Saint Nicholas, all without a border. The cookie dough is pressed into the mold and, once unmolded, the cookie "mirrors" the mold. You can use springerle molds, if you like.*

❅ **LIFESPAN** *2 weeks at room temperature in airtight container*

Yield: *sixty 3-inch cookies*

❅ INGREDIENTS

4 cups all-purpose flour
1 teaspoon baking powder
1 cup (2 sticks) unsalted butter, softened
2 cups firmly packed light brown sugar
2 teaspoons finely grated lemon zest
2 teaspoons ground cinnamon

½ teaspoon freshly grated nutmeg
¼ teaspoon ground cloves
½ teaspoon almond extract
2 large eggs
2 tablespoons milk, if needed
¼ cup sliced natural almonds, chopped

❅ DIRECTIONS

1. Whisk flour and baking powder together in a small bowl.

2. In a large bowl with an electric mixer on medium-high speed, beat butter until creamy, about 2 minutes. Add brown sugar gradually, beating until light and fluffy, about 3 minutes; beat in lemon zest, spices, and almond extract. Add eggs one at a time, beating well after each. Add about one-third of flour and mix on low speed. Gradually add remaining flour, mixing just until blended. Add milk if necessary to make a smooth, pliable dough; it should not be sticky. Turn dough out onto work surface and knead in almonds. Divide dough in half and wrap both pieces in plastic wrap. Refrigerate until firm enough to handle without sticking, about 1 hour.

3. Preheat oven to 350 degrees F. Line 2 cookie sheets with parchment paper.

4. Generously sprinkle *speculaas* molds with flour, then press dough into molds. Scrape off any excess dough with flat edge of icing spatula or a knife. Rap edge of mold on counter and cookie should begin to release. Rap again if necessary. Flour molds in between each cookie. Place cookies 2 inches apart on cookie sheets.

5. Bake until just beginning to color, about 20 minutes. Timing will depend on size and thickness of molds or cutters. Slide parchment onto racks to cool cookies completely.

GOOD COOKIE TIP

Sometimes working with the dough and molds can be tricky—and frustrating—if the dough sticks to the molds. An alternate technique would be to roll out the dough to about ¼-inch thickness and to press molds into dough. For complete instructions in this vein, turn to the Springerle recipe on page 144. Or roll out to ¼-inch thickness and cut out cookies with cutters. Baking times will vary depending on size and thickness of cookies.

Easy Christmas Wreaths

✳ **TYPE** *Drop cookie* ✳ **HABITAT** *United States*

✳ **DESCRIPTION** *These easy, crunchy, no-bake wreath-shaped candies are colorful and great to make with kids. With just four ingredients, you get a lot of bang for your buck.*

✳ **FIELD NOTES** *Cornflakes have been used in many an American cookie and candy recipe—Americans have a way with convenience foods!*

✳ **LIFESPAN** *1 week at room temperature or 1 month refrigerated in airtight container; best stored in single layers separated by waxed paper*

Yield: *30 wreaths*

❄ INGREDIENTS

20 ounces white chocolate, broken into pieces

1 teaspoon green liquid food coloring

5 cups cornflake cereal, crushed

3 tablespoons cinnamon red-hot candies

❄ DIRECTIONS

1. Line 2 cookie sheets with parchment paper and coat with nonstick spray.

2. Melt chocolate in microwave or top of double boiler over simmering water; stir until smooth. Stir in food coloring, then stir in corn flakes until evenly mixed.

3. Drop onto cookie sheets by generously rounded tablespoon 1 inch apart. Dip a chopstick in warm water, stick down in center of each mound, and make circular motions until you create a hole and a wreath is formed. While still moist, arrange red-hot candies on the wreaths to mimic holly berries, using 3 or 5 per wreath. Place sheets in refrigerator until wreaths are cooled and firm.

Fig Cookies · *Cucidati*

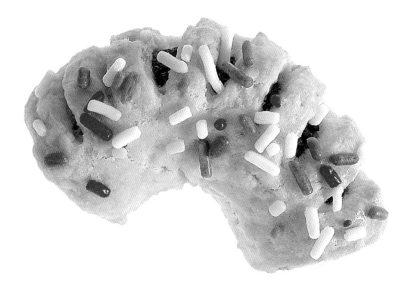

❄ **TYPE** *Filled cookie*   ❄ **HABITAT** *Italy*

❄ **DESCRIPTION** *These cookies feature a tender rolled pastry filled with a sophisticated filling moist with figs, but also flavored with apricot, raisins, candied peel, vanilla, cinnamon, and cloves. The crunchy, coarse-sugar topping is elegant; the multicolored nonpareil version is fun and festive—your choice. The cookies do take time to make, but none of the steps are complicated. Note that the 100 percent apricot fruit spread used in the filling is less sweet than apricot jam, so please be sure to buy the correct ingredient.*

❄ **FIELD NOTES** *The name* cucidati *is the Sicilian version of* buccellati, *which means "little bracelets." Indeed, the semicircular cookies could be said to resemble a fancy bracelet. This is my version, as I found all of the classic fillings to be quite dry. My technique of cooking the figs with sugar and water might not be traditional, but it yields a moister, tastier filling.*

❄ **LIFESPAN** *2 weeks at room temperature in airtight container*

Yield: *75 cookies*

❄ **INGREDIENTS**

Dough:
4 cups all-purpose flour
½ cup granulated sugar
1 teaspoon baking powder
1 teaspoon salt
¾ cup (1½ sticks) chilled unsalted butter, cut into tablespoons
¼ cup chilled vegetable shortening, cut into pieces
4 large eggs

Filling:
2 cups dried whole Calimyrna figs (about 14), halved and stemmed
1½ cups water

½ cup granulated sugar
½ cup blanched or natural whole almonds
⅓ cup dark raisins
⅓ cup golden raisins
¼ cup 100 percent apricot spreadable fruit
¼ cup diced candied orange peel
½ teaspoon vanilla extract
½ teaspoon ground cinnamon
¼ teaspoon ground cloves

Topping:
1 large egg
Coarse sugar
Multicolored nonpareils or sprinkles

❄ **DIRECTIONS**

1. Pulse flour, sugar, baking powder, and salt together in food processor. With the machine on, add butter and shortening a few pieces at a time through feed tube and process until evenly combined and mixture resembles coarse meal. Pulse in eggs one at a time until mixture forms large, moist clumps. Scrape dough onto large piece of plastic wrap, cover completely with wrap, and refrigerate for 1 hour or overnight.

2. To make filling, combine figs, water, and sugar in a medium saucepan and bring to a boil over medium-high heat. Reduce heat to low, cover, and simmer until figs are fork tender, about 20 minutes. Transfer to food processor and process into a thick, smooth paste. Add almonds and process until nuts are finely chopped within the paste. Add remaining filling ingredients and pulse until combined. (Filling can be made up to 4 days ahead and refrigerated in airtight container.)

3. Preheat oven to 350 degrees F. Line 2 cookie sheets with parchment paper.

4. Divide dough into 8 pieces. Shape each piece by rolling beneath your palms on a lightly floured surface into 1-inch-diameter rope; then roll rope out flat with a rolling pin to a ¼-inch thickness, about 3 inches wide and 20 inches long. Spread filling down center, making a 1-inch-wide x ½-inch-thick strip of filling. Fold both sides over the filling and pinch firmly to close. Use hands to squeeze the cylinder gently and roll back and forth to coax into a round shape; have seam side down. Make slashes at ¼-inch intervals all along the pastry, then cut into 3-inch lengths. Place 1 inch apart on cookie sheets and bend into a crescent shape. Repeat with remaining dough and filling.

5. To make topping, whisk egg until frothy. Brush egg on cookies and sprinkle with coarse sugar, sprinkles, or nonpareils. Bake until light golden brown around edges and on bottom, about 20 minutes. Slide parchment onto racks to cool cookies completely.

Filled Cream Cheese Pastries
Sutemeny

❄ **TYPE** *Filled cookie*   ❄ **HABITAT** *Hungary*

❄ **DESCRIPTION** *These flaky cream-cheese pastries can be made with your choice of filling. The apricot and poppy seed filling recipes will both make enough filling all by themselves for the quantity of dough made here, but I can't resist making both kinds. Any leftover filling can be spread onto toast or folded into morning oatmeal.*

❄ **FIELD NOTES** *This recipe comes courtesy of family friend Carolyn Laychak. Fruit and poppy seed pastries such as these are very popular in Hungary; sometimes the pastry is yeast risen, but this is much easier.*

❄ **LIFESPAN** *3 days at room temperature loosely wrapped in foil; after storing, they improve when warmed gently in a 250-degree F oven*

Yield: *65 pastries*

❄ INGREDIENTS

Dough:
2½ cups all-purpose flour
1 cup (2 sticks) chilled unsalted butter
One 8-ounce package cold cream cheese

Apricot filling (about 1½ cups):
12 ounces dried apricots
1½ cups water
⅓ cup granulated sugar
1½ teaspoons fresh lemon juice

Poppy seed filling (about 1½ cups):
¾ cup poppy seeds

¾ cup milk
5 tablespoons dark raisins, chopped
1½ tablespoons unsalted butter
5 tablespoons granulated sugar
5 tablespoons honey
3 tablespoons sliced almonds, finely chopped
½ teaspoon finely grated lemon zest

Egg wash:
1 large egg
1 teaspoon water

❄ DIRECTIONS

1. Combine dough ingredients in a large bowl and beat with an electric mixer on low speed until moist clumps form. Knead with hands just until smooth on lightly floured work surface. Cover with plastic and refrigerate until firm enough to roll out, at least 2 hours or overnight.

2. Meanwhile, make filling(s). *For apricot filling,* combine apricots, water, and sugar in a medium saucepan and bring to a boil. Reduce heat to medium-low and simmer, stirring occasionally, until apricots are tender and liquid has evaporated by about half, about 10 minutes. Let cool slightly, then process in food processor until smooth. Pulse in lemon juice. Mixture should be thick enough to hold a shape when dropped from a spoon. If too thin, scrape back into saucepan and cook over medium-low heat until thickened, stirring constantly. Let cool to room temperature before using.

   For poppy seed filling, grind poppy seeds in a clean coffee or spice grinder, or place in a zipper-lock plastic bag and crush with a rolling pin. Transfer to a medium saucepan; add milk,

   raisins, butter, sugar, honey, and almonds, and stir. Bring to a boil, cover, reduce heat to medium-low, and simmer, stirring occasionally, until thick enough to mound when dropped by a spoon, about 15 minutes. Stir in lemon zest. Let cool to room temperature before using.

3. Preheat oven to 350 degrees F. Line 2 cookie sheets with parchment paper.

4. Roll dough out to ¼-inch thickness on lightly floured surface and cut into 2-inch squares. Spread each with ½ teaspoon filling, leaving a ¼-inch border of dough all around; fold one corner into the center, brush top of that corner with water, then fold opposite corner in toward center to form a diamond shape. Press the second corner down on moistened corner to seal, pinching if necessary; these do have a tendency to unfold during baking.

5. Transfer to cookie sheets, 2 inches apart. Whisk egg and water together in a small bowl and brush each pastry with it. Bake until light golden brown, about 25 minutes. Slide parchment onto racks to cool cookies completely.

Gingerbread, Baseler
Basler Leckerli

❄ **TYPE** *Bar cookie*   ❄ **HABITAT** *Switzerland*

❄ **DESCRIPTION** *This spicy bar cookie is made in one saucepan and starts with boiling honey. This unusual technique gives it a very chewy texture, so do not expect a soft, cakey bar. These have substance and lots of flavor from the Kirschwasser (clear cherry brandy), candied citrus peel, honey, almonds, and spices. These improve in texture and flavor after a few days, so plan ahead.*

❄ **FIELD NOTES** *Leckerli is the Swiss-German word for gingerbread, finding its root in the adjective* lecker, *meaning delicious, which is also where the German noun* Leckerei, *delicacy or choice morsel, comes from. Basel is a beautiful old city in the German-speaking area of Switzerland, and Basler Leckerli have a long tradition there. Kirschwasser, which flavors the bar and the icing, is a favorite of the Swiss. You only need a little bit, but you can use the rest of the bottle for other Swiss dishes, such as fondue, in which its inclusion is traditional.*

❄ **LIFESPAN** *Up to 6 days at room temperature in airtight container, but at their best after 3 or 4 days*

68

Yield: *35 bars*

❄ **INGREDIENTS**

Bars:
4 cups all-purpose flour
1 teaspoon baking soda
2 teaspoons ground cinnamon
½ teaspoon freshly grated nutmeg
¼ teaspoon ground cloves
Pinch of salt
1¼ cups honey
1 cup granulated sugar
⅓ cup Kirschwasser

¼ cup minced candied lemon peel
¼ cup minced candied orange peel
½ cup whole natural almonds, coarsely
  chopped
½ cup sliced natural almonds

Glaze:
1 cup confectioners' sugar, sifted
1 tablespoon water
2 teaspoons Kirschwasser
¼ teaspoon vanilla extract

❄ **DIRECTIONS**

1. Coat a 9 x 13-inch baking pan with nonstick spray.

2. Whisk flour, baking soda, spices, and salt together in a small bowl.

3. Combine honey and granulated sugar in a medium saucepan and bring to a boil, swirling pan a few times to combine mixture. Boil for 2 minutes; make sure sugar is dissolved. Remove from heat and allow to cool for 2 minutes.

Whisk in Kirschwasser (be careful, as mixture may bubble up). Stir in candied peels and almonds, then stir in flour mixture. Scrape into baking pan, spreading batter evenly. Allow to sit for 1 hour; the texture and flavor improve with time.

4. Preheat oven to 325 degrees F. Bake until light golden brown and a toothpick inserted in center comes out clean, about 30 minutes. Place pan on rack to cool. Cut into 35 bars (5 x 7) before glazing, but leave in pan.

5. Meanwhile, whisk together glaze ingredients in a small bowl. Spread in a thin, even layer over cooled bars. Rescore bars while glaze is warm; glaze will crack if you try to cut it after cooling.

GOOD COOKIE TIP

To fancy these up, slice candied cherry halves and use these and bits of candied fruit or nuts to make designs on each bar. You can make somewhat abstract flower shapes or just create a little cluster of candied fruit to add color in a pretty pattern.

Gingerbread, Honey
Honiglebkuchen

❋ **TYPE** *Rolled cookie*   ❋ **HABITAT** *Germany*

❋ **DESCRIPTION** *This is just one of many spiced cookie doughs that are popular in Western Europe. This rolled cookie can be cut into any shape before baking and glazing; you can even purchase a special Santa-shaped cutter and decorative papers featuring a colorful Saint Nicholas, which can be affixed after baking (see Resources). Note that there is no butter or fat in the dough, which yields an unusual chewy texture; it also means you should take care not to overcook them, as they will dry out.*

❋ **FIELD NOTES** *The word* Lebkuchen *means gingerbread, and this honey version, which is very popular, dates back to the fourteenth century, when honey was the sweetener of choice. Honey also provides some moisture, which might be lacking from the absence of butter in the recipe. Special guilds (groups) specialized in baking* Lebkuchen, *particularly in the city of Nuremberg, which, not surprisingly, was on the spice-trade route and produced a prodigious amount of honey.*

❋ **LIFESPAN** *1 month at room temperature in airtight container in single layers separated by waxed paper; best if allowed to age at least a few days before eating*

Yield: *forty-five 2-inch cookies*

❄ INGREDIENTS

Cookies:

3 cups all-purpose flour

½ teaspoon baking soda

1 teaspoon ground cinnamon

½ teaspoon ground cloves

½ teaspoon ground ginger

¼ teaspoon ground cardamom

½ cup blanched whole almonds, finely ground in food processor

½ cup (3 ounces) finely minced mixed candied fruit

¾ cup firmly packed dark brown sugar

¾ cup honey

1 large egg

Glaze:

½ cup confectioners' sugar, sifted

1½ teaspoons hot water, as needed

½ teaspoon almond extract

½ teaspoon vanilla extract

Nonpareils (optional)

❄ DIRECTIONS

1. Whisk flour, baking soda, spices, ground almonds, and minced candied fruit together in a medium bowl.

2. In a large bowl with an electric mixer on medium-low speed, beat together brown sugar, honey, and egg until combined, about 1 minute. Add about one-third of flour mixture and mix on low speed. Gradually add remaining flour mixture, mixing just until moist clumps form. Cover with plastic wrap and refrigerate until firm enough to roll out, about 1 hour or overnight.

3. Preheat oven to 350 degrees F. Line 2 cookie sheets with parchment paper.

4. Roll dough out to ¼-inch thickness between lightly floured pieces of parchment paper. Peel off top paper and cut out shapes of your choice; I like to use a 2½-inch acorn-shaped cookie cutter. Place at least 2 inches apart on cookie sheets.

5. Bake until a little bit puffed and just beginning to turn light golden brown around the edges, about 13 minutes. Slide parchment onto racks to cool cookies for 5 minutes.

6. While cooling, prepare glaze. Whisk together confectioners' sugar, water, and extracts until smooth. Glaze should be thin enough to brush on the cookies, but not too runny. Add more water if too thick, or more sugar if too thin. Brush over cookies with a pastry brush while still warm. For acorns, I brush just the top halves to look like the "cap" of the acorn. Sprinkle nonpareils over warm glaze, if using, before it dries. Allow cookies and glaze to cool completely.

GOOD COOKIE TIP

If you use Santa cutters, they will be larger than the cookie cutters suggested above, so you will get fewer cookies and the baking time will be a little longer. To affix the Santa papers, simply cool the cookies, brush with a little glaze, and press the papers on top of the glaze, which will act like a glue.

Gingerbread People

❄ **TYPE** *Rolled cookie*   ❄ **HABITAT** *United States*

❄ **DESCRIPTION** *I like these dark, spicy gingerbread cookies cut into people shapes and decorated with cinnamon red-hot candy eyes and mouths affixed with dabs of royal icing. For alternatives, refer to the directions and recipes for Classic Rolled Sugar Cookies (page 148) and Iced Sugar Cookies (page 150) for other decoration ideas using colored sugar and royal icing. If you like a crisper gingerbread cookie, roll these out a bit thinner and bake an extra minute. For a thicker, chewier cookie, follow the instructions and make sure not to overbake.*

❄ **LIFESPAN** *3 weeks at room temperature in airtight container*

Yield: *forty-five 3-inch cookies*

❄ INGREDIENTS

3¼ cups all-purpose flour
1 teaspoon baking soda
¼ teaspoon salt
1 cup (2 sticks) unsalted butter, softened
¾ cup firmly packed dark or light brown sugar
2 teaspoons ground ginger
1 teaspoon ground cinnamon

¼ teaspoon freshly grated nutmeg
¼ teaspoon ground cloves
½ cup unsulphured molasses
1 large egg

Decoration:
Thick Royal Icing (page 151)
Cinnamon red-hot candies

❄ DIRECTIONS

1. Whisk flour, baking soda, and salt together in a small bowl.

2. In a large bowl with an electric mixer on medium-high speed, beat butter until creamy, about 2 minutes. Add brown sugar gradually, beating until light and fluffy, about 3 minutes; beat in spices. Beat in molasses and egg, beating well after each. Add about one-third of flour and mix on low speed. Gradually add remaining flour, mixing just until blended. Scrape dough onto large piece of plastic wrap. Use wrap to help shape into a large, flat disc, then cover with wrap. Refrigerate until firm enough to roll out, at least 2 hours or overnight.

3. Preheat oven to 350 degrees F. Line 2 cookie sheets with parchment paper.

4. Roll dough out to ¼-inch thickness on lightly floured surface. Cut out ginger-bread people or any other shape of your choice. Place 2 inches apart on cookie sheets. Place similar-sized cookies on same sheet.

5. Bake until just light golden brown around edges and the edges feel dry and firm to touch, about 12 minutes, depending on size. Cool in pans on racks for a few minutes, then transfer cookies to racks to cool completely.

6. For decorations, place royal icing in a parchment cone, snip a tiny opening, and pipe small dots of icing where you would like the cinnamon red-hot candies to go. I suggest eyes and a mouth for both men and women. Then, give the men three candies down their fronts, like buttons on a shirt, and a string of candies around the women's waists to define their skirts. Allow icing to harden and dry, which will act as glue for the candies.

GOOD COOKIE TIP

To make particularly realistic, and adorable, gingerbread people, use a clean—very clean—garlic press to press out strands of hair with the dough. Brush the head area with some beaten egg, then arrange the "hair" as you like on their heads before baking. For a simpler approach to the decoration, place red-hot candies on the cookies before baking by just pressing into the dough. If you're lucky, the cookie will bake around them and hold them in place, but this doesn't always work.

Ginger Crackle Cookies

※ **TYPE** *Shaped cookies*   ※ **HABITAT** *United States*

※ **DESCRIPTION** *These gingerbread-like cookies have a crackled appearance, hence their name, and an extra-crunchy, coarse-sugar topping. I have chosen to make these in one large log, which is then sliced like big, thick biscotti. This gives you an alternate shape to the many round cookies in your holiday repertoire, but if you like, you can roll these into 1½-inch balls, dip the tops in the coarse sugar, and bake them for about 12 minutes.*

※ **FIELD NOTES** *Many early American cookbooks, or "receipt" books, have recipes for similar spicy molasses cookies. Molasses was a common and inexpensive sweetener and frequently used in desserts.*

※ **LIFESPAN** *1 week at room temperature in airtight container*

Yield: *60 cookies*

❄ INGREDIENTS

4 cups all-purpose flour
1 teaspoon baking soda
1 teaspoon salt
1 cup (2 sticks) unsalted butter, softened
1 cup granulated sugar
1¼ cup unsulfured molasses

1½ teaspoons ground ginger
1 teaspoon ground cinnamon
½ teaspoon freshly grated nutmeg
½ teaspoon ground cloves
2 large eggs
Coarse sugar

❄ DIRECTIONS

1. Whisk the flour, baking soda, and salt together in a small bowl.

2. In a large bowl with an electric mixer on medium-high speed, beat butter until creamy, about 2 minutes. Add granulated sugar gradually, beating until light and fluffy, about 3 minutes; beat in molasses and spices. Add eggs one at a time, beating well after each. Add about one-third of flour mixture and mix on low speed. Gradually add remaining flour, mixing just until blended. Dough may be loose. Cover with plastic wrap and refrigerate until firm enough to roll into ropes, at least 2 hours or overnight.

3. Preheat oven to 350 degrees F. Line 2 cookie sheets with parchment paper.

4. Divide dough into 8 pieces and roll each beneath your palms on a lightly floured surface into a 1-inch-wide x 15-inch-long rope. Sprinkle some coarse sugar on work surface and roll rope over sugar to coat about half its circumference. Place 2 ropes on each cookie sheet, sugar side up and several inches apart.

5. Bake until puffed and dry to the touch, about 18 minutes. A toothpick inserted in the center should come out clean. Slide parchment onto racks to cool cookies completely. Cut each log crosswise into 1¼-inch-thick cookies.

Ginger Snaps ❉ *Pepparkakor*

❊ **TYPE** *Rolled cookie*   ❊ **HABITAT** *Sweden*

❊ **DESCRIPTION** *Filled with cinnamon, ginger, cloves, cardamom, molasses, and orange zest, these rolled cookies will thrill all gingerbread lovers. Use any shape cookie cutter that you like.*

❊ **FIELD NOTES** *These are my friend Joan Eckert's Swedish grandmother Olivia Abrahamsson's cookies, and they are typical of Swedish ginger snaps. This version is extra spicy, flavorful, and easy to work with.*

❊ **LIFESPAN** *2 weeks at room temperature in airtight container*

Yield: *one hundred 3-inch cookies*

❄ INGREDIENTS

3½ cups all-purpose flour
I teaspoon baking soda
½ cup (I stick) unsalted butter, softened
¾ cup granulated sugar
I½ teaspoons ground cinnamon
I½ teaspoons ground ginger

I teaspoon ground cloves
¼ teaspoon ground cardamom
I large egg
¾ cup unsulfured molasses
2 teaspoons finely grated orange zest

❄ DIRECTIONS

1. Whisk flour and baking soda together in a small bowl.

2. In a large bowl with an electric mixer on medium-high speed, beat butter until creamy, about 2 minutes. Add sugar gradually, beating until light and fluffy, about 3 minutes. Beat in spices, then beat in egg, molasses, and orange zest until well blended. Add about one-third of flour mixture and mix on low speed. Gradually add remaining flour, mixing just until blended. Scrape dough onto large piece of plastic wrap. Use wrap to help shape into 3 flat discs, then cover completely with wrap. Refrigerate overnight to allow flavors to develop.

3. Preheat oven to 375 degrees F. Line 2 cookie sheets with parchment paper.

4. Roll out one disc at a time to ⅛-inch thickness on lightly floured surface; you may need to flour the rolling pin too. Make sure they are rolled out this thinly, as the quality—the "snap"—of the finished cookie depends on it. Cut out

cookies with cutters and place 1 inch apart on cookie sheets. Repeat with remaining dough.

5. Bake until dry and light golden brown on bottom and can be gently lifted from the sheet, about 9 minutes. Let cool on sheets on racks for a couple of minutes, then carefully transfer to racks to cool completely.

GOOD COOKIE TIP

These cookies can be made into placecards for your holiday family meal. Simply cut out large simple shapes, such as leaves, and use a parchment cone (page 12) filled with Thick Royal Icing (page 151) or melted chocolate (page 10) to write the names of your guests. For a fancier effect, dissolve a bit of edible gold powder in a drop or two of vodka and use a soft artist's brush to write guests' names on the cookies.

Honey Balls · *Struffoli*

❊ **TYPE** *Shaped cookie*   ❊ **HABITAT** *Italy*

❊ **DESCRIPTION** *These are tiny nuggets of dough coated with a sweet honey glaze.*

❊ **FIELD NOTES** *Rose Liuzzo from Modica, Sicily, handed this recipe down to her daughter, Mary, who in turn gave it to her son, Robert Agro, who generously shared it with me. Thank you to all the generations! All of the recipes that I have seen for* struffoli *deep-fry the dough. Bob suggested baking for the lighter touch his family now enjoys. Directions for both techniques are included. The recipe also suggests forming a pyramid shape with the* struffoli, *which is classic, but you can also form them into a wreath shape on a large round platter and place a pillar candle in the center. A dessert and table decoration in one!*

❊ **LIFESPAN** *Best served soon after they are made*

Yield: *20 servings*

❄ INGREDIENTS

Dough:
- 3½ cups all-purpose flour
- ¼ cup granulated sugar
- 1½ teaspoons baking powder
- ¼ teaspoon salt
- 4 large eggs
- ½ cup light vegetable oil (such as sunflower, safflower, canola)
- 1 teaspoon vanilla extract
- 2 quarts light vegetable oil for frying (optional)

Coating:
- 1 cup honey
- ¼ cup granulated sugar
- ½ cup diced candied citron
- Nonpareils

❄ DIRECTIONS

1. In a large bowl, whisk together flour, sugar, baking powder, and salt. Whisk eggs, ½ cup oil, and the vanilla together in a small bowl. Add wet mixture to the dry, and mix with an electric mixer on low speed until moist clumps begin to form. Allow dough to rest for 10 minutes.

2. If baking, preheat oven to 350 degrees F. Line 2 cookie sheets with parchment paper. If frying, heat 2 quarts oil in a deep-fat fryer or heavy, deep pot to 375 degrees F.

3. Take a handful of dough at a time and roll beneath your palms on a lightly floured surface into ½-inch-diameter ropes. Cut into ½-inch lengths.

4. If *baking*, place dough pieces 2 inches apart on cookie sheets and bake until light golden brown, about 13 minutes. Slide parchment onto racks to cool cookies completely. Gently place cookies in a large bowl; set aside. (May be stored at room temperature in airtight container up to 2 days.)

   If *frying*, place about a dozen pieces of dough in the hot oil at a time, stirring a few times to prevent sticking. Fry until light golden brown, about 2 minutes. Remove with a slotted spoon, drain on paper towels, then gently place cookies in a large bowl.

5. Up to 4 hours before serving, place honey and sugar in a small saucepan over medium heat; stir to combine and bring to a boil, swirling pan occasionally. Allow to boil for 1 minute, remove from heat, then stir in citron. Gently pour over cookies in bowl and fold carefully with a large rubber spatula. The syrup might not immediately stick to cookies. Keep folding, and as it cools it will become stickier and coat cookies well. Mound honey-coated *struffoli* on a plate, forming a small pyramid. Sprinkle with nonpareils and serve within 4 hours. Guests eat by picking off cookies with their fingers and popping directly into their mouths.

NOTE: *The recipe makes many, many, tiny balls of pastry, so the yield is better understood by suggesting how many people can share the dish than by the number of cookies.*

Honey Caramel Pecan Bars

✳ **TYPE** *Bar cookie*   ✳ **HABITAT** *United States*

✳ **DESCRIPTION** *These bar cookies feature a shortbread crust and delectable, gooey, caramel-like topping packed with pecan halves.*

✳ **FIELD NOTES** *Pecan bars of all sorts crop up in southeastern United States cookbooks. One notation said the original was from Williamsburg, but of course that's what Virginians are gonna say!*

✳ **LIFESPAN** *1 week at room temperature in airtight container*

Yield: *40 bars*

❄ INGREDIENTS

Crust:
2½ cups all-purpose flour
¼ teaspoon salt
1 cup (2 sticks) unsalted butter, softened
½ cup granulated sugar
½ teaspoon vanilla extract

Filling:
1 cup (2 sticks) unsalted butter
1 cup firmly packed light brown sugar
1 cup honey
⅓ cup heavy cream
¼ teaspoon vanilla extract
Pinch of salt
3 cups pecan halves

❄ DIRECTIONS

1. Coat a 9 x 13-inch baking pan with nonstick spray.

2. Whisk flour and salt together in a small bowl.

3. In a large bowl with an electric mixer on medium-high speed, beat butter until creamy, about 3 minutes. Add granulated sugar gradually, beating on high speed until light and fluffy; this may take as long as 8 minutes. Do not rush; mixture should be almost white in color. Beat in vanilla. Add about one-third of flour mixture and mix on low speed. Gradually add remaining flour, mixing just until blended. Pat crust in an even layer into baking pan. Refrigerate 30 minutes or overnight.

4. Preheat oven to 350 degrees F. Bake crust until just light golden brown around edges and center is dry but not fully cooked, about 20 minutes.

5. Meanwhile, prepare filling. Place butter, brown sugar, and honey in a medium saucepan and cook over medium heat, stirring occasionally, until butter melts. Increase heat to high, bring to a boil, and let boil for 5 minutes. Remove from heat and stir in heavy cream, vanilla, salt, and pecans. Pour filling over partially baked crust and bake until filling has darkened and edges have set, about 30 minutes. Center will still be slightly wet.

6. Set pan on rack to cool completely, preferably overnight. Cut into 40 bars (5 x 8).

Honey Molasses Peanut Butter Popcorn Balls

❄ **TYPE** *Shaped confection*   ❄ **HABITAT** *United States*

❄ **DESCRIPTION** *These might not be cookies, but they are sweet, easy-to-make treats that are welcome at any Christmas party—and you can tie ribbons around them and hang them on your tree. If you have a candy thermometer, this recipe will be easier, but I have given you directions to follow if you don't.*

❄ **LIFESPAN** *4 days at room temperature in airtight container*

Yield: *18 popcorn balls*

❄ INGREDIENTS

Popcorn balls:

½ cup unpopped popcorn (or 12 cups popped)

1 tablespoon light vegetable oil (such as sunflower, safflower, canola)

¼ cup honey

¼ cup unsulfured molasses

¼ cup smooth, salted, natural (not hydrogenated) peanut butter

1 cup granulated sugar

Decoration:

12 yards ¼-inch ribbon (optional), cut into 24-inch pieces

❄ DIRECTIONS

1. Place popcorn and oil in a large pot over high heat. Partially cover to allow steam to escape. When you hear first kernels popping, cover pot and shake back and forth occasionally. Keep over heat until all popping stops. Listen to popping; it will eventually slow down and when it completely stops, immediately pour popcorn into a large bowl.

2. Whisk together honey, molasses, and peanut butter in a small saucepan until smooth. Stir in sugar; place over high heat and bring to a boil, swirling pan a few times to help mixture blend. Cook until mixture reaches 260 degrees F on a candy thermometer (if you drip a bit of mixture into a glass of cold water, it will form a hard ball). Remove from heat and immediately pour over popcorn. Quickly stir to thoroughly coat corn before syrup hardens too much; it should still be warm to touch.

3. Scoop up a handful of coated popcorn (about ½ cup, but you can do this by eye) and compress into a ball about 2 inches across. Set on rack to cool. If desired, tie ribbon around each ball with center of ribbon on center bottom of ball, knot at the top (there will be two long ends), then knot ends together. You will have a large loop for slipping over tree boughs.

Honey Walnut Cookies
Melomakarona

❄ **TYPE** *Filled cookie*   ❄ **HABITAT** *Greece*

❄ **DESCRIPTION** *According to fellow International Association of Culinary Professionals (IACP) member Aglaia Kremezi, these are the traditional Greek Christmas cookie. Some have nuts in the batter, but the best, such as these based upon her recipe, have a spiced nut filling. After baking they are soaked in a honey syrup, which adds flavor, sweetness, and moistness. Plan ahead, because these cookies are best if allowed to sit at least overnight before eating.*

❄ **FIELD NOTES** *Some researchers date these back to the Phoenicians. We do know for sure that honey was a popular sweetener in ancient times.*

❄ **LIFESPAN** *2 weeks at room temperature in airtight container in single layers separated by waxed paper*

Yield: *40 cookies*

❄ INGREDIENTS

Dough:
4 cups all-purpose flour
2½ teaspoons baking powder
1½ cups fine semolina flour
1 teaspoon ground cinnamon
1 teaspoon ground cloves
1¼ cups light olive oil
⅓ cup granulated sugar
1 cup fresh orange juice
½ cup brandy
2 teaspoons finely grated lemon zest
2 teaspoons finely grated orange zest

Filling:
3 cups walnut halves, toasted (page 11)
and finely chopped
1 tablespoon plus 1 teaspoon ground
cinnamon

Syrup:
1½ cups water
1 cup honey
1 cup granulated sugar

❄ DIRECTIONS

1. Whisk flour, baking powder, semolina, cinnamon, and cloves together in a medium bowl.

2. In a large bowl, whisk together oil and sugar vigorously to blend well. Whisk in orange juice, brandy, and citrus zests. Add about one-third of flour mixture and mix with an electric mixer on low speed. Gradually add remaining flour, mixing just until blended. Continue to beat on medium speed until a soft, smooth dough is formed, about 2 minutes. Cover with plastic wrap and let dough rest for 30 minutes at room temperature.

3. To make filling, toss together walnuts and cinnamon in a medium bowl. Preheat oven to 350 degrees F. Line 2 cookie sheets with parchment paper.

4. Take pieces of dough the size of a small egg and roll between your palms into ovals about 2½ inches long. Make a hole with your finger in the bottom and stuff about 1 teaspoon of filling inside. Pinch dough tightly to seal in filling. Place on cookie sheets seam side down about 2 inches apart. Reshape pastries into oval, if needed. Repeat with remaining dough and filling; there will be filling left over.

5. Bake until just light golden brown around edges, about 25 minutes.

   Meanwhile, make syrup. Stir together water, honey, and sugar in a small saucepan over medium-high heat, and bring to a boil. Reduce heat to medium-low and simmer 10 minutes; keep warm.

6. Place hot cookies in a large, shallow heatproof bowl or rimmed platter in a single layer and gently pour warm syrup evenly over all. Allow to sit for 15 minutes; turn cookies over to further absorb syrup, and let cool completely. One by one, roll cookies in remaining nut filling and place on rack to dry for 10 minutes before placing in a container to ripen overnight.

Jeweled Fruit Bars · *Muzurkas*

❄ **TYPE** *Bar cookie*   ❄ **HABITAT** *Poland*

❄ **DESCRIPTION** *These bar cookies have grated orange zest and almonds in the crust and a rich jewel-toned topping of apricots, dates, figs, raisins, candied citrus peels, and nuts. All of the fruits and nuts in the topping should be about ⅓ inch in size; don't chop them too finely or you will lose their individual colors and textures in the final cookie.*

❄ **FIELD NOTES** *My friend Mary McNamara's mother-in-law, Angie Czajkowski, shared this recipe with me. They both live in Hadley, Massachusetts, which has a large Polish population. Angie, who got the recipe from Hadley neighbor Alvira Balut, always makes these on Christmas Eve, and says they freeze up to 1 month in an airtight container.*

❄ **LIFESPAN** *4 days at room temperature in airtight container*

Yield: *24 bars*

❄ **INGREDIENTS**

Crust:
- 1 cup all-purpose flour
- 3 tablespoons finely ground almonds
- ⅔ cup unsalted butter, softened
- ⅔ cup granulated sugar
- ½ teaspoon finely grated orange zest
- 2 large eggs

Topping:
- 4 teaspoons cornstarch
- 4 teaspoons granulated sugar
- 1 cup orange juice
- ½ cup diced dried apricots
- ½ cup diced dates
- ¼ cup diced dried Calimyrna figs
- ¼ cup dark or golden raisins
- 2 tablespoons diced candied lemon peel
- 2 tablespoons diced candied orange peel
- ½ cup chopped natural almonds

❄ **DIRECTIONS**

1. Preheat oven to 350 degrees F. Coat a 9 x 13-inch baking pan with nonstick spray.

2. Whisk flour in a small bowl. Stir in ground almonds.

3. In a large bowl with an electric mixer on medium-high speed, beat butter until creamy, about 2 minutes. Add sugar gradually, beating until light and fluffy, about 3 minutes; beat in orange zest. Add eggs one at a time, beating well after each. Add about one-third of flour mixture and mix on low speed. Gradually add remaining flour mixture, mixing just until blended. Scrape dough into baking pan and smooth evenly with an offset spatula. Bake until very light golden brown and a toothpick inserted in center comes out clean, about 17 minutes.

4. Meanwhile, make topping. Whisk together cornstarch and sugar in a small saucepan. Whisk in orange juice until dry mixture is dissolved. Stir in apricots, dates, figs, raisins, and citrus peels. Place over medium heat and bring to a simmer, stirring often. Once simmering, stir constantly until thickened; you should be able to draw the spoon along bottom of pan and see pan. Remove from heat and stir in almonds. Spread topping evenly over crust. Bake until light golden brown around edges and topping is set (it will look a bit dull), about 18 minutes.

5. Place pan on rack to cool. Cut into 24 bars (4 x 6).

Kris Kringle's Chocolate Krinkles

❄ **TYPE** *Shaped cookie*   ❄ **HABITAT** *United States*

❄ **DESCRIPTION** *Fudgy, easy, yummy, these cookies are rolled in either confectioners' sugar or cocoa (or half the batch in each) and, after baking, the dark chocolate–colored cookie cracks through the topping and creates a crackled appearance. No further decoration is needed. Kids are fascinated by the change that takes place as they bake.*

❄ **FIELD NOTES** *I first came across these cookies in the 1980s, and I have seen many variations, some featuring fresh mint, cinnamon, orange, or coffee. I decided to go for straight, unadulterated chocolate, and I am sure you will love the results.*

❄ **RELATED SPECIES** Orange Chocolate Krinkles: *Add 2 teaspoons finely grated orange zest to sugar-egg mixture;* Cinnamon Chocolate Krinkles: *Add ½ teaspoon ground cinnamon to sugar-egg mixture.*

❄ **LIFESPAN** *2 weeks at room temperature in airtight container*

Yield: *80 cookies*

❄ INGREDIENTS

5 ounces unsweetened chocolate, broken
　into pieces
½ cup (1 stick) unsalted butter
2 cups all-purpose flour
2 teaspoons baking powder
¼ teaspoon salt

4 large eggs
2 cups granulated sugar
1 teaspoon vanilla extract
Confectioners' sugar
Natural unsweetened cocoa powder

❄ DIRECTIONS

1. Melt chocolate and butter together in top of a double boiler over simmering water or in microwave until about three-quarters melted. Remove from water or microwave and stir until completely melted and smooth.

2. Meanwhile, stir flour, baking powder, and salt together in a medium bowl.

3. In a large bowl with an electric mixer on high speed, beat eggs, granulated sugar, and vanilla together until creamy, about 2 minutes. Whisk chocolate-butter mixture until smooth, and beat into egg mixture until smooth. Add about one-third of flour mixture and mix on low speed. Gradually add remaining flour, mixing just until blended. Dough may be very thin; that's okay because it will firm up upon cooling. Cover with plastic wrap and refrigerate until firm enough to roll into balls, at least 6 hours or overnight.

4. Preheat oven to 350 degrees F. Line 2 cookie sheets with parchment paper. Sift some confectioners' sugar into a small bowl. Sift some cocoa into another small bowl.

5. Roll dough between your palms into 1-inch balls, then roll in either confectioners' sugar or cocoa to coat completely (I do half the batch in sugar, the other half in cocoa). Place balls 2 inches apart on cookie sheets and gently flatten just enough so they don't roll.

6. Bake until puffed and crackled in appearance, and surface is dry to touch, about 12 minutes; centers will still feel somewhat soft. You should be able to gently lift edge of a cookie up from sheet with a metal spatula. Slide parchment onto racks to cool cookies completely.

Linzer Stars

⁂ **TYPE** *Rolled cookies*   ⁂ **HABITAT** *Austria*

⁂ **DESCRIPTION** *The classic linzertorte is a spiced-nut pastry filled with jam and is found all over Austria. Every bakery and many a home baker have their own versions, but nuts, spices, and lemon zest usually figure into the mix, as does a dark red jam, such as black currant or raspberry. This is a cookie version.*

⁂ **FIELD NOTES** *The torte dates back to the 1700s, but the cookie is no doubt a variation of the tart-like original and a somewhat newer creation.*

⁂ **LIFESPAN** *Best served day they are made, arranged in a single layer on a serving plate*

Yield: *24 large star-shaped cookies and 12 small stars*

❊ INGREDIENTS

2½ cups all-purpose flour
1 cup skinned whole hazelnuts or
   blanched whole almonds (5 ounces)
⅔ cup granulated sugar
1 teaspoon ground cinnamon
¼ teaspoon ground cloves
¼ teaspoon salt

1 cup (2 sticks) unsalted butter, cut into
   tablespoons
¼ teaspoon almond extract
1 teaspoon finely grated lemon zest
1 cup seedless red or black currant or
   raspberry jam
Confectioners' sugar

❊ DIRECTIONS

1. Pulse the flour, nuts, granulated sugar, cinnamon, cloves, and salt together in a food processor until nuts are finely ground. With machine on, add butter a few pieces at a time through feed tube and process until evenly combined. Pulse in almond extract and lemon zest until mixture begins to form large, moist clumps. Scrape dough onto large piece of plastic wrap, form into 2 very flat discs, cover completely with plastic wrap, and refrigerate until firm enough to roll out, at least 2 hours or overnight.

2. Preheat oven to 325 degrees F. Line 2 cookie sheets with parchment paper.

3. Roll 1 disc out to ¼-inch thickness on floured surface; you may need to flour the pin too. Cut out large stars and place at least 1 inch apart on cookie sheet. Cut out a small star from the center of half the cookies and place on separate cookie sheet. Repeat with remaining dough.

4. Bake just until light golden brown around the edges, about 10

minutes for small stars, 20 minutes for larger stars. Cool on sheets on racks for a couple of minutes, then carefully transfer to racks to cool completely. (Cookies may be stored in an airtight container up to 2 weeks.)

5. On the day of serving, place jam in a small bowl and stir until smooth. Using a small offset spatula, spread a thin layer of jam on the flat bottoms of the large solid star cookies and on the bottom of half the small star cookies; you will have some jam leftover. Place large cutout star cookies and remaining small stars on cookie sheet, top side up. Use a fine-mesh strainer to sieve confectioners' sugar over them. Carefully sandwich the cookie tops with cookie bottoms, large stars with large and small with small, confectioners' sugar side up. Small stars are ready to eat. For larger stars, place remaining jam in parchment paper cone, snip off the tip, and carefully pipe into star-shaped windows to fill up the cutout space.

GOOD COOKIE TIP

For Valentine's Day, make these in heart shapes. They can also be made in simple round shapes, in which case a fluted edge looks nice.

Macaroons, Chocolate
Macarons au Chocolat

✳ **TYPE** *Piped cookie*　　✳ **HABITAT** *France*

✳ **DESCRIPTION** *These tiny morsels simply burst with bittersweet chocolate flavor, and the mingling textures of the chewy, tender cookies sandwiching silky dark chocolate ganache are simply sublime. These are works of art.*

✳ **FIELD NOTES** *French-style macaroons are an obsession for Parisians, with several patisseries vying at once to be deemed the place to purchase these sweets.*
They come in a simple almond flavor as well as pistachio, strawberry, raspberry, coffee, and even rose. But the chocolate ones seem to be in a class by themselves.
I knew someone who went to Paris just to taste her way through the chocolate macaroons that the City of Lights had to offer. Okay, that person was me, but that should not diminish the point!

✳ **LIFESPAN** *Filled, 1 day; unfilled, 1 week at room temperature in airtight container*

Yield: *54 cookies*

❄ INGREDIENTS

Cookies:
 1½ cups blanched whole almonds
 2¼ cups confectioners' sugar, sifted
 3 tablespoons Dutch-processed
   unsweetened cocoa powder
 3 large egg whites
 ⅛ teaspoon cream of tartar

Filling:
 4 ounces bittersweet chocolate, broken
   into pieces
 ⅔ cup heavy cream

❄ DIRECTIONS

1. Preheat oven to 400 degrees F. Line 2 cookie sheets with parchment paper.

2. Place almonds and 1½ cups of confectioners' sugar in a food processor and pulse to combine, then process until nuts are as finely ground as possible; this could take several minutes. Mixture should be powdery. Pulse in cocoa.

3. In a large, clean, grease-free bowl, whip egg whites with an electric mixer on high speed until foamy. Add cream of tartar and beat until soft peaks form. Add remaining ¾ cup confectioners' sugar and beat until stiff but not dry peaks form. Fold nut mixture into meringue. Scrape mixture into a pastry bag fitted with ½-inch round tip (such as Ateco #806). Pipe 1-inch rounds 2 inches apart onto cookie sheets. Allow to sit for 10 minutes so that the "kiss" shapes begin to settle into smooth rounds.

4. Bake until dry to touch and you can lift one from parchment without it breaking, about 10 minutes; tops may look crackled, which is okay. Slide parchment onto racks to cool cookies completely.

5. For filling, place chocolate in a heatproof bowl. Bring heavy cream to a boil in a small saucepan and pour over chocolate. Let sit for a few minutes, then whisk until smooth. Stir over ice until thick enough to spread or refrigerate until spreading consistency is reached, about 1 hour. Using a pastry bag fitted with a coupler and a small star tip (such as Ateco #18), pipe a swirl of ganache onto half the cookies on their flat bottoms. Alternatively, use a small offset spatula to spread the ganache. Top each cookie with another one to make a ganache sandwich, flat bottom to flat bottom.

Macaroons, Pine Nut
Amaretti ai Pignoli

❋ **TYPE** *Piped cookies* ❋ **HABITAT** *Italy*

❋ **DESCRIPTION** *Small, chewy, and intensely almond-flavored, the concentrated flavor and wonderful texture of these cookies come from almond paste. Pine nuts, which have a very rich, buttery flavor and texture, stud the tops. These cookies are piped, so you do need a pastry bag and a ½-inch round tip, but they are very easy to make.*

❋ **FIELD NOTES** *Almond paste has been a favorite ingredient in Europe for hundreds of years, and the Italians put it to many uses, including these traditional macaroons. *Amaretti *means "little bitter things," which refers to the bitter almonds used to make the paste. Bitter almonds are still used abroad, but here in the United States we use canned almond paste to approximate the texture and flavor of European almond paste. The paste packaged in a tube from the supermarket just won't do, so go to a specialty shop or mail-order the canned variety (some supermarkets do stock it).*

❋ **RELATED SPECIES** Double Almond Macaroons: *Sprinkle tops with (or dip in) sugar and press a blanched whole almond in center, broad side down, instead of covering with pine nuts. Bake as directed.*

❋ **LIFESPAN** *2 weeks at room temperature in airtight container*

Yield: *32 cookies*

❈ INGREDIENTS

1 pound canned almond paste
2 cups granulated sugar

4 large egg whites
1½ cups pine nuts

❈ DIRECTIONS

1. Preheat oven to 325 degrees F. Line 2 cookie sheets with parchment paper and coat lightly with nonstick spray.

2. In a large bowl, break almond paste into large pieces. With an electric mixer on medium speed, beat until paste is broken into pea-sized pieces. Add sugar and beat until combined, about 1 minute. Add egg whites one at a time, beating well after each. Beat until creamy and lightened, about 3 minutes. Scrape mixture into pastry bag fitted with ½-inch round tip (such as Ateco #806). Pipe rounds about 1½ inches in diameter and 1 inch high (they will look like chocolate kisses) onto cookie sheets 1 inch apart.

3. Place pine nuts in a small bowl. One by one, gently lift each cookie (use your index and middle finger to scoop them up) and invert into bowl of pine nuts (cookies are a little sticky, so they will cling to your fingers when you invert them, allowing you some control). The nuts will stick to top of cookie. Return each cookie, nut side up, to sheet. If you cannot lift cookies because they are too sticky, simply press the pine nuts on top.

4. Bake until light golden brown around the edges and on bottom and just beginning to brown on top, about 20 minutes. Slide parchment onto racks to cool cookies completely.

Meringues, Chocolate Walnut

❄ **TYPE** *Drop cookie*   ❄ **HABITAT** *United States*

❄ **DESCRIPTION** *These are the cookies I mentioned in the book's introduction—my first-ever memorized recipe, which I make again and again. These are easy and quick to make and combine sweet, crunchy vanilla-scented meringue with toasted walnuts and dark chocolate morsels.*

❄ **FIELD NOTES** *My mom found this recipe in a church cookbook, where they were called Surprise Meringues. The surprise is that you only see a hint of the chocolate and nuts inside the cookie; when you bite into them, there is an explosion of flavor and textures.*

❄ **LIFESPAN** *2 weeks at room temperature in airtight container*

Yield: *45 cookies*

❄ INGREDIENTS

2 large egg whites
⅛ teaspoon cream of tartar
¾ cup granulated sugar
1 teaspoon vanilla extract

1 cup semisweet chocolate chips
¼ cup walnut halves, toasted (page 11)
and finely chopped

❄ DIRECTIONS

1. Preheat oven to 275 degrees F. Line 2 cookie sheets with parchment paper.

2. In a medium, clean, grease-free bowl with an electric mixer on high speed, whip egg whites until foamy. Add cream of tartar and whip until soft peaks form. Add sugar gradually, whipping until stiff but not dry peaks form. Beat in vanilla. Fold in chocolate chips and walnuts. Drop by generously rounded teaspoon 2 inches apart on cookie sheets.

3. Bake until completely firm and dry, but still white, about 25 minutes; you should be able to lift cookies from pan. Slide parchment onto racks to cool cookies completely.

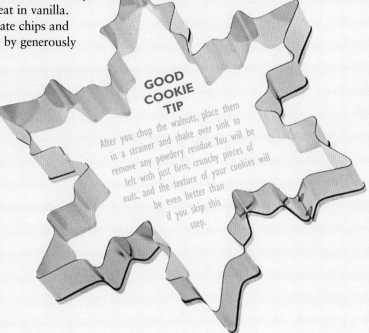

GOOD COOKIE TIP

After you chop the walnuts, place them in a strainer and shake over sink to remove any powdery residue. You will be left with just firm, crunchy pieces of nuts, and the texture of your cookies will be even better than if you skip this step.

Meringue Mushrooms
Champignons en Meringue

❋ **TYPE** *Piped cookie*   ❋ **HABITAT** *France*

❋ **DESCRIPTION** *These crispy meringue cookies are just amazing. They really look like mushrooms, especially when piled in a basket like you just harvested them; they fool my guests every time, to the delight of children and adults alike.*

❋ **FIELD NOTES** *The classic French Christmas dessert is* bûche de Noël, *which is a rolled cake decorated to resemble a log. And to embellish the log, pastry chefs often make meringue mushrooms to go along with the woodland theme.*

❋ **LIFESPAN** *2 weeks at room temperature in airtight container*

Yield: *36 mushrooms*

❋ INGREDIENTS

4 large egg whites
½ teaspoon cream of tartar
1 cup granulated sugar
1 teaspoon vanilla extract

Dutch-processed unsweetened cocoa powder
3 ounces bittersweet or semisweet chocolate

❋ DIRECTIONS

1. Preheat oven to 225 degrees F. Line 2 cookie sheets with parchment paper.

2. In a large, clean, grease-free bowl with an electric mixer on high speed, whip egg whites until foamy. Add cream of tartar and whip until soft peaks form. Add sugar gradually, whipping until stiff but not dry peaks form. Beat in vanilla. Scrape mixture into pastry bag fitted with ½-inch round tip (such as Ateco #806).

3. On one cookie sheet, pipe about 36 rounds that vary in size from 1 to 2 inches in diameter (like white mushrooms from the supermarket) about 1 inch apart. Cookies will have peaked tops, like chocolate kisses; that's okay. Dip your index finger in water and gently press down on peak to make a rounded, mushroom-like top. Place cocoa in a fine-mesh strainer and sift lightly over rounds. It should look like the mushroom tops are dusted with dirt.

4. On other cookie sheet, pipe out stems as follows: hold tip directly over pan with tip's opening facing straight down. Begin applying pressure; the meringue stem will touch the pan and you should immediately lift pastry bag straight up to guide stem straight up. When stem is about 1 inch high, gradually lessen your pressure and pull up. You should have an upright stem with a peaked top. Just like with caps, you want 36 stems, and they should vary in height and thickness a little bit to match up with the varying sizes of caps.

5. Bake until completely dry and crispy to touch, about 1½ hours. Slide parchment onto racks to cool cookies completely. Take a very small, sharp paring knife and cut off peaked tops of stems to create a flat surface; this is the surface that will attach to cap. The meringue is so dry that you can almost scrape it flat with the knife after cutting off the peak to create a nice, smooth surface.

6. Temper the chocolate according to directions on page 10. Take a small offset spatula and spread a little bit of chocolate on the bottom of a cap very neatly, going all the way to edges but not onto sides of cap. Take a stem that visually matches in size (you just pick and choose caps and stems that seem to go together; remember, there is a lot of variation in real mushrooms). Affix cut side of stem in center of wet chocolate and press to adhere. Place upright (stem side down, cap side up) on a cookie sheet or on its side if stem is already connected pretty firmly. Repeat with all mushrooms, and place on pan. Allow chocolate to harden completely (you may place pan in refrigerator briefly if chocolate is not firming up).

Mincemeat Pies with Irish Whiskey

❄ **TYPE** *Filled cookie*   ❄ **HABITAT** *Ireland*

❄ **DESCRIPTION** *This recipe is based on a mincemeat recipe given to me by Darina Allen and her Ballymaloe Cookery School in Cork, Ireland. Darina sometimes uses beef suet; I opted to make this a vegetarian version using butter. It is jam-packed with raisins, currants, and citrus peels and enlivened with Irish whiskey. Start one week ahead to allow the mincemeat to mature. Use a Golden Delicious or Gala apple. Darina likes to serve these with a dollop of whiskey-flavored whipped cream.*

❄ **FIELD NOTES** *Making traditional mincemeat, which usually included beef as well as beef suet, was a way to preserve the meat for future use. The amount of fat and alcohol in the mixture helped the mincemeat last a long, long time.*

❄ **LIFESPAN** *Best served day they are made*

Yield: *22 pastries*

❄ INGREDIENTS

Mincemeat filling:
  1 apple, peeled, cored, and diced
  1 cup (2 sticks) unsalted butter, softened
  2 cups firmly packed dark brown sugar
  1 cup dark raisins
  ¾ cups golden raisins
  ¾ cup dried currants
  2 tablespoons fresh lemon juice
  2 tablespoons orange marmalade
  1 tablespoon finely grated lemon zest
  1 tablespoon minced candied citron
  1 tablespoon minced candied lemon peel
  1 tablespoon minced candied orange peel
  ¼ cup Irish whiskey

Pastry:
  2 cups all-purpose flour
  Pinch of salt
  1 tablespoon confectioners' sugar
  ¾ cups (1½ sticks) chilled unsalted butter,
    cut into tablespoons
  1 large egg, beaten until frothy

Topping:
  1 large egg
  1 teaspoon water
  Confectioners' sugar

❄ DIRECTIONS

1. Combine mincemeat ingredients except the whiskey in a large saucepan. Bring to a boil, stirring occasionally. Reduce heat to medium-low and simmer 15 minutes, stirring occasionally. Mixture will thicken and raisins will swell. Stir in whiskey and simmer 5 more minutes. Let cool to room temperature, stirring occasionally to release heat, then scrape into airtight container and refrigerate 1 week to mature the flavors. You may make the pastries right away, but the taste will not be quite as rich.

2. To make pastry, place flour, salt, and confectioners' sugar in food processor and pulse to combine. With machine on, add butter a few pieces at a time through feed tube and process until evenly combined. With machine still on, slowly pour in beaten egg and process just until dough comes together in moist clumps; you may not need the whole egg. Place dough on large piece of plastic wrap, then use wrap to help shape into a large flat disc and cover completely with wrap. Refrigerate until firm enough to roll out, about 1 hour.

3. Preheat oven to 350 degrees F. Line 2 cookie sheets with parchment paper. Whisk egg and water until frothy.

4. Roll dough out to ⅛-inch thickness on lightly floured surface, and cut 3-inch circles. Place 1 teaspoon filling on bottom half of each round. Brush edges with egg wash, then fold over to create a half-moon shape. Crimp edges together with tines of a fork. Brush egg wash all over pastry and place 2 inches apart on cookie sheets. Cut out small holly leaves from dough scraps and roll tiny bits of dough into holly berries. Place on top of pastries; the egg wash will help them adhere. You may brush the "holly" with egg wash as well.

5. Bake until light golden brown around edges, about 20 minutes. Slide parchment onto racks and allow to cool for 5 minutes. Sprinkle with confectioners' sugar while still warm.

Moravian Ginger Cookies

✳ **TYPE** *Rolled cookie*   ✳ **HABITAT** *United States*

✳ **DESCRIPTION** *These are paper-thin, crispy, elegant ginger-molasses cookies. The dough is easy to make, but to get the results that make these so spectacular, you must take the time to roll them out as thin as possible. Just when you think they are as thin as they can get, roll them out some more! The low oven temperature gives you the characteristic crispy cookies with an even color and no browning—just luscious crunch! The classic shape is a scalloped round about 3 inches across.*

✳ **FIELD NOTES** *These cookies hail from a Protestant sect that flourished in the mid-1400s throughout Poland, Bohemia, and Moravia, which is where their name comes from. An excellent version of these cookies is produced commercially, and this homemade version is almost exactly the same. There is a section of Winston-Salem, North Carolina, called Old Salem where a group of German immigrants established a homestead in 1766. The original recipe used in Old Salem, which was given to me by North Carolina native Lou Currin, made over 500 cookies! Lou is an excellent baker and she said this was the recipe to use; she also says she keeps the dough in the refrigerator for up to three weeks at a time, just rolling out what she needs for freshly baked cookies.*

✳ **LIFESPAN** *2 weeks at room temperature in airtight container*

Yield: *one hundred and fifty 3-inch cookies (at least!)*

❄ INGREDIENTS

3 to 3½ cups all-purpose flour, as needed

3 tablespoons unsalted butter, melted

3½ tablespoons vegetable shortening, melted

1 cup unsulfured molasses

½ cup firmly packed light brown sugar

1½ teaspoons ground cinnamon

1½ teaspoons ground cloves

1½ teaspoons ground ginger

1½ teaspoons baking soda

2 tablespoons boiling water

❄ DIRECTIONS

1. Whisk flour in a small bowl.

2. Combine melted butter and shortening in a large bowl and beat with an electric mixer on low speed to combine, about 30 seconds. Add molasses and brown sugar and beat until creamy, about 2 minutes; beat in spices. Dissolve baking soda in boiling water and beat into batter. Add about one-third of flour and mix on low speed. Gradually add a total of 3 cups flour, mixing just until blended. Dough should be firm but soft and not sticky. You will be rolling it out on a generously floured surface, so do not make it too stiff, but add more flour, if necessary. Scrape dough onto large piece of plastic wrap. Use wrap to help shape into a large, flat disc, then cover with wrap. Allow to sit at room temperature overnight for flavor and texture to develop.

3. Preheat oven to 275 degrees F. Line 2 cookie sheets with parchment paper.

4. Roll out ¼ cup dough at a time as thin as paper on a generously floured surface, moving the dough around frequently to keep it from sticking. It is vitally important that you take the time to roll this dough out as thinly as suggested. Cut out scalloped rounds, or any other shape, and place about 1 inch apart on cookie sheets.

5. Bake until dry and firm to touch, but not at all browned, about 10 minutes. Cookies might give a bit in the center when pressed with your finger, but will firm up tremendously upon cooling. Slide parchment onto racks to cool cookies completely.

Nanaimo Bars

✳ **TYPE** *Bar cookie*   ✳ **HABITAT** *Canada*

✳ **DESCRIPTION** *These are sticky, gooey, very sweet bars layered with nuts, coconut, chocolate, graham cracker crumbs, and sweetened condensed milk and are named for the city in British Columbia.*

✳ **FIELD NOTES** *These are thought to have originated in their namesake city. According to my Canadian friend and food expert, Nathan Fong, some say the original recipe might have appeared in the* Nanaimo Hospital Cookbook *in the late 1950s. Others peg the recipe as much older, appearing in the 1930s in the* Vancouver Sun *newspaper, where they were called Chocolate Refrigerator Cakes. Nathan also says that the original had a sweet sugary, creamy filling, but I think they are sweet and rich enough as presented here. They are also sometimes referred to as Magic Bars, possibly because they are magically easy to make, and occasionally as Hello Dollies, but I have no idea why!*

✳ **LIFESPAN** *1 week at room temperature in airtight container*

Yield: *25 bars*

❄ INGREDIENTS

½ cup (1 stick) unsalted butter

1 cup graham cracker crumbs (made from 8 whole crackers)

1 cup walnut halves, finely chopped

1¼ cups bittersweet or semisweet chocolate chips

1 cup sweetened flaked coconut

One 14-ounce can sweetened condensed milk

❄ DIRECTIONS

1. Preheat oven to 350 degrees F.

2. Place butter in 8-inch square baking pan; put pan in oven until butter melts. Sprinkle graham cracker crumbs evenly over melted butter, stir with a spoon to combine, then pat crumbs into an even layer. Sprinkle walnuts evenly over crumb layer, then sprinkle chocolate chips evenly over nuts. Sprinkle coconut evenly over chocolate chips, then pour condensed milk evenly over all.

3. Bake until medium golden brown around edges and light golden brown all over the top, about 25 minutes. Middle will look a little loose; that's okay. Place pan on rack to cool. Cut into 25 bars (5 x 5).

Night Before Christmas Mice

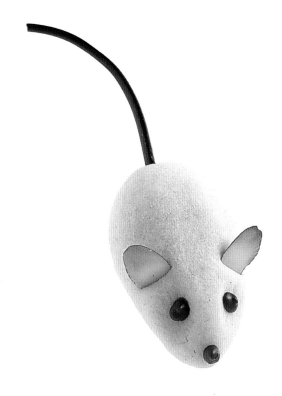

❄ **TYPE** *Shaped cookies*   ❄ **HABITAT** *United States*

❄ **DESCRIPTION** *These beguiling little sugar-cookie mice have chocolate eyes and noses, almond ears, and licorice tails. They are the ultimate in crafty Christmas cookies and delight all who see them perched on the edge of a cookie plate.*

❄ **FIELD NOTES** *Many, many years ago I was in a specialty shop in New York City and saw tiny chocolate mice with chocolate-covered almond ears and colorful silk tails. Larry Burdick, an amazing chocolatier, was responsible for them and, before I knew it, I was seeing articles and mentions of these mice everywhere. These are my cookie version and a tribute to the original.*

❄ **LIFESPAN** *2 weeks at room temperature in airtight container stored in a single layer*

Yield: *40 mice*

❄ INGREDIENTS

Cookies:
3 cups all-purpose flour
¼ teaspoon salt
I cup (2 sticks) unsalted butter, softened
¾ cup granulated sugar
I teaspoon almond or vanilla extract
I large egg

Decoration:
Sliced natural almonds
10 feet red or black licorice laces (thin,
spaghetti-like strands), cut into 3-inch
lengths
6 ounces semisweet chocolate, melted and
kept slightly warm

❄ DIRECTIONS

1. Whisk flour and salt together in a small bowl.

2. In a large bowl with an electric mixer on medium-high speed, beat butter until creamy, about 2 minutes. Add sugar gradually, beating until light and fluffy, about 3 minutes; beat in extract. Beat in egg. Add about one-third of flour mixture and mix on low speed. Gradually add remaining flour, mixing just until blended. Scrape dough onto large piece of plastic wrap and cover completely with wrap. Refrigerate until firm enough to roll into balls, at least 2 hours or overnight.

3. Preheat oven to 350 degrees F. Line 2 cookie sheets with parchment paper.

4. Roll pieces of dough between your palms into 1¼-inch ovals. Slightly elon- gate one side to form nose. Gently pinch bridge of nose to form eye sockets. Place 2 sliced almonds behind eyes, inserting as shown in photograph to make ears. Place mice 2 inches apart on cookie sheets.

5. Bake until light golden brown on bottom and around edges, about 15 minutes. Place pans on racks and immediately insert skewer into mouse's rounded posterior, going in about ½ inch. Remove skewer and insert length of licorice for tail as far as it will go. It will wedge in and adhere to the still-warm cookie. Place melted chocolate in parchment cone and snip tiny opening. Pipe small chocolate eyes and nose in appropriate places. Place sheet in refrigerator until chocolate has firmed up.

Nutmeg Logs

✳ **TYPE** *Shaped cookie*   ✳ **HABITAT** *United States*

✳ **DESCRIPTION** *These log-shaped cookies are redolent with freshly grated nutmeg and spiked with a hint of rum. The silky dough is very easy to work with and you don't even have to chill it before forming the logs. Instead of rolling these cookies on a floured surface, you sprinkle the surface with sugar, which gives the cookies a little crunch and a tad more sweetness.*

✳ **FIELD NOTES** *Here is another recipe from good friend Joan Eckert; these are from an old neighbor of hers, Alice Ross Bennett Remy. Once Joan tasted these at Alice's home, she knew she had to have the recipe—and now you have it too. Alice is no longer with us, but wherever she is, she can rest assured that her tradition of baking is being carried on.*

✳ **LIFESPAN** *1 week at room temperature in airtight container*

Yield: *40 logs*

❄ **INGREDIENTS**

Cookies:

3 cups all-purpose flour
¼ teaspoon salt
1 cup (2 sticks) unsalted butter, softened
¾ cup granulated sugar, plus more for sprinkling
1 tablespoon light or dark rum
1½ teaspoons freshly grated nutmeg
1 teaspoon vanilla extract
1 large egg

Frosting:

6 tablespoons (¾ stick) unsalted butter, softened
2 cups confectioners' sugar, sifted
2 tablespoons heavy cream
2 teaspoons light or dark rum
1 teaspoon vanilla extract

2 teaspoons freshly grated nutmeg

❄ **DIRECTIONS**

1. Preheat oven to 350 degrees F. Line 2 cookie sheets with parchment paper.

2. Whisk flour and salt together in a small bowl.

3. In a large bowl with an electric mixer on medium-high speed, beat butter until creamy, about 2 minutes. Add granulated sugar gradually, beating until light and fluffy, about 3 minutes; beat in rum, nutmeg, and vanilla. Beat in egg. Add about one-third of flour mixture and mix on low speed. Gradually add remaining flour, mixing just until blended. Take a handful of dough at a time and shape into a log by rolling it under your palms on a sugared surface into ½-inch-diameter ropes. Cut ropes into 3-inch lengths. Place logs 2 inches apart on cookie sheets. Bake until light golden brown on bottom and around edges, about 13 minutes.

4. Meanwhile, make frosting. In a medium bowl with mixer on medium-high speed, beat the butter until creamy, about 3 minutes. Add confectioners' sugar, heavy cream, rum, and vanilla and beat until creamy, about 2 minutes.

5. Place cookie sheets on racks to begin cooling. Immediately, while cookies are still warm, spread them with icing, using a small offset spatula. The icing, which is thick and fluffy, will melt and adhere to cookie (it will harden upon cooling, allowing you to layer these cookies in a tin or mail them, if desired). Sprinkle with nutmeg while icing is still wet. Allow cookies to cool and icing to harden before serving.

Peanut Butter Chocolate Kiss Cookies

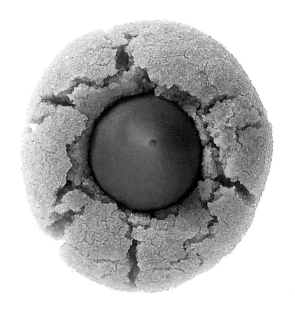

✳ **TYPE** *Shaped cookie*   ✳ **HABITAT** *United States*

✳ **DESCRIPTION** *These feature peanut butter cookie dough with a milk chocolate kiss nestled in the center. Kids love to make 'em and eat 'em!*

✳ **LIFESPAN** *2 weeks at room temperature in airtight container in a single layer*

Yield: *34 cookie kisses*

❄ INGREDIENTS

1¼ cups all-purpose flour
1 teaspoon baking soda
½ teaspoon salt
½ cup (1 stick) unsalted butter, softened
1 cup smooth, unsalted, natural (not hydrogenated) peanut butter

½ cup granulated sugar, plus more for coating
½ cup firmly packed light brown sugar
½ teaspoon vanilla extract
1 large egg
34 milk chocolate kisses, unwrapped

❄ DIRECTIONS

1. Whisk flour, baking soda, and salt together in a small bowl.

2. In a large bowl with an electric mixer on medium-high speed, beat butter and peanut butter together until creamy, about 2 minutes. Add both sugars and beat until light and fluffy, about 3 minutes; beat in vanilla. Add egg and beat until smooth. Add about one-third of flour mixture and mix on low speed. Gradually add remaining flour, mixing just until blended. Scrape dough onto large piece of plastic wrap. Use wrap to help shape into a large, flat disc, then cover completely with wrap.

   Refrigerate until firm enough to roll into balls, at least 1 hour or overnight.

3. Preheat oven to 350 degrees F. Line 2 cookie sheets with parchment paper.

4. Roll dough between your palms into 1½-inch balls, roll in granulated sugar to coat completely, and place 2 inches apart on cookie sheets. Gently flatten just enough so they don't roll off.

5. Bake just until light golden brown on bottoms (peek to check), about 18 minutes. Press chocolate kiss into center of each cookie (they might crack; that's okay) and return to oven for 1 minute. Cool cookies on sheets on racks for a couple of minutes, then carefully transfer to racks to cool completely.

Pecan Butter Balls

✻ **TYPE** *Shaped cookie*   ✻ **HABITAT** *United States*

✻ **DESCRIPTION** *These cookies combine ground pecans, sweet butter, confectioners' sugar, and vanilla into a delectable snow-white ball.*

✻ **FIELD NOTES** *Many countries have variations of this cookie (Mexican wedding cakes, for instance, are the same) and for good reason—they're packed with ingredients that are addictively good. These are popular throughout the United States, but particularly in the Southeast, where pecans are harvested.*

✻ **LIFESPAN** *2 weeks at room temperature in airtight container in layers separated by waxed paper*

Yield: *34 balls*

❄ INGREDIENTS

¾ cup pecan halves
2 cups confectioners' sugar
¼ teaspoon salt

1 cup (2 sticks) unsalted butter, softened,
 cut into tablespoons
1 teaspoon vanilla extract
2 cups all-purpose flour

❄ DIRECTIONS

1. Pulse pecans, ½ cup confectioners' sugar, and the salt together in a food processor to break up nuts, then process until nuts are finely ground. Add butter a few pieces at a time, pulsing to incorporate, then process until mixture is smooth; pulse in vanilla. Add flour, pulse until incorporated, then process until dough begins to form a ball. Scrape dough onto large piece of plastic wrap and form into a very flat disc, cover completely in wrap, and refrigerate until firm enough to roll into balls, at least 2 hours or overnight.

2. Preheat oven to 350 degrees F. Line 2 rimmed cookie sheets with parchment paper.

3. Roll dough into 1-inch balls between your lightly floured palms and place 2 inches apart on cookie sheets. Gently flatten just enough so they don't roll off. Bake until light golden brown around edges, about 15 minutes.

4. Cool on sheets on racks for 5 minutes, then sift remaining 1½ cups confectioners' sugar over warm cookies. After cookies have cooled completely, roll them in the confectioners' sugar on the sheet to cover completely.

Peppernuts *Pfeffernusse*

❊ **TYPE** *Shaped cookie*   ❊ **HABITAT** *Germany*

❊ **DESCRIPTION** *This is a classic spiced holiday cookie, filled with nuts and candied citrus peels. The dough is rolled out into ropes, which are cut into small nuggets, so don't be put off by the high yield; the work goes fast and folks eat these a handful at a time. They greatly improve with age, so do not skip that step.*

❊ **FIELD NOTES** *These German cookies have several distinguishing characteristics. They are flavored with pepper, either white or black, among other spices, and the cookie dough is allowed to dry overnight before baking. Also, many modern renditions use butter to make a softer, richer cookie. This is a classic recipe, which, while crunchier, allows for very long storage—a real benefit at Christmastime.*

❊ **LIFESPAN** *1 month at room temperature in airtight container*

Yield: *185 tiny cookies*

❄ INGREDIENTS

Cookies:
2¾ cups all-purpose flour
⅓ cup whole blanched almonds
¼ cup diced candied lemon peel
¼ cup diced candied orange peel
½ teaspoon baking powder
¼ teaspoon salt
¼ teaspoon white or black pepper
1 teaspoon ground cinnamon
¼ teaspoon ground cardamom

⅛ teaspoon ground cloves
3 large eggs
1 cup firmly packed light brown sugar

Topping:
Confectioners' sugar, sifted
or
2 cups confectioners' sugar, sifted
2 teaspoons vanilla extract
5 teaspoons hot water, or as needed

❄ DIRECTIONS

1. Place flour and almonds in food processor and process until nuts are finely ground and powdery. Add candied peels and pulse until peels are finely minced. Pulse in baking powder, salt, pepper, and spices.

2. Combine eggs and brown sugar in a large bowl and whisk vigorously until thick and creamy, about 3 minutes. Add about one-third of flour mixture, stirring with a wooden spoon. Add remaining flour mixture, stirring just until combined and dough begins to come away from sides of bowl. Scrape dough onto large piece of plastic wrap and form dough into 2 very flat discs, cover completely with wrap, and refrigerate until firm enough to roll into ropes, at least 2 hours or overnight.

3. Line 2 cookie sheets with parchment paper.

4. Take a handful of dough at a time and roll it beneath your palms on a lightly floured surface into a ½-inch-diameter rope. Cut each rope into 1-inch lengths. Place 1 inch apart on cookie sheets. Allow to ripen at room temperature overnight.

5. Preheat oven to 350 degrees F. Bake until light golden brown around edges, about 15 minutes. Slide parchment onto racks. If using just confectioners' sugar, place it in a bowl and toss warm cookies in to coat, then transfer to rack to cool completely.

   Alternatively, whisk together confectioners' sugar, vanilla, and enough hot water in a small bowl to form a very fluid glaze. Dip tops of cookies in glaze, then place glaze side up on racks to cool completely.

6. Ripen cookies at least 1 week by storing in an airtight container along with a slice of apple. Store in small groups of about 2 cups each for every slice of apple so that the moisture provided by the fruit is effective.

Pistachio Cranberry Biscotti

❋ **TYPE** *Shaped cookie*   ❋ **HABITAT** *United States and Italy*

❋ **DESCRIPTION** *These biscotti are speckled with pale green pistachios and dark red dried cranberries. Don't leave out the lemon zest or extracts, as they really add flavor. Biscotti deliberately have a dry texture, which gives them an extreme crunchiness that takes quite nicely to a cup of tea or coffee—just dunk them in!*

❋ **FIELD NOTES** *The word* biscotti *means "twice cooked" in Italian, and indeed these cookies are baked, sliced, and baked again. Nowadays you can't go into an American coffeehouse without finding a couple of versions; untraditional flavors, such as the recipe here, are very American. Classic Italian versions often feature anise and/or almonds and are frequently dunked in sweet wine.*

❋ **LIFESPAN** *1 month at room temperature in airtight container*

Yield: *65 biscotti*

❊ INGREDIENTS

Biscotti:

2 cups all-purpose flour
⅔ cup granulated sugar
½ teaspoon baking powder
½ teaspoon baking soda
3 large eggs
2 teaspoons finely grated lemon zest
1 teaspoon almond extract

1 teaspoon vanilla extract
½ cup unsalted natural pistachios, toasted (page 11) and roughly chopped
½ cup dried cranberries

Topping:

1 large egg, beaten
½ cup granulated sugar
1 tablespoon ground cinnamon

❊ DIRECTIONS

1. Whisk flour, sugar, baking powder, and baking soda together in a large bowl. Add eggs one at a time and, with an electric mixer on low speed, beat until well mixed. Beat in lemon zest and extracts, then beat in pistachios and cranberries. Cover with plastic wrap and refrigerate until firm enough to roll, at least 30 minutes.

2. Preheat oven to 350 degrees F. Line 2 cookie sheets with parchment paper. To make topping, whisk egg in small bowl. Stir together sugar and cinnamon in separate bowl.

3. Divide dough into even thirds and shape each piece by rolling on a lightly floured surface into a log about 2 inches in diameter and 15 inches long. Place 2 logs on one cookie sheet, the third on the other. Brush logs with beaten egg and sprinkle with cinnamon-sugar mixture.

4. Bake until puffed, dry to the touch, and light golden brown around edges and on top, about 30 minutes. Remove from oven and let cool 2 minutes by setting pans on racks.

5. One by one, gently remove each log to a cutting board. Slice the biscotti very thinly, about ¼ inch thick, on diagonal, making the biscotti about 5 inches long. Return slices to cookie sheets, standing them up on their "bottoms," not their broad sides, and spacing them about ¼ inch apart. Bake again until completely dry and very light golden brown, about 20 minutes. Slide parchment onto racks to cool cookies completely.

Pizzelle

❋ **TYPE** *Pressed cookie*   ❋ **HABITAT** *Italy*

❋ **DESCRIPTION** *This large, decorative, thin, waffle-like cookie is made with a pizzelle maker. This special griddle embosses the cookies as they cook. (I use a VillaWare nonstick pizzelle maker; see Resources.) The cookies are flavored with lemon zest and anise, and can be left whole or cut into quarters while still warm. They can also be rolled into cones to be filled with whipped cream or pressed into muffin cups to cool as edible baskets for ice cream.*

❋ **FIELD NOTES** *While it is possible to flavor pizzelle any number of ways (with spices, citrus, nuts), you will very often find them in Italy made with anise. They are pronounced "peet-SELL-ay."*

❋ **LIFESPAN** *1 week at room temperature in airtight container*

Yield: 15 pizzelle

❄ INGREDIENTS

2 cups all-purpose flour
1 teaspoon baking powder
¼ teaspoon salt
2 large eggs
¾ cup granulated sugar

2 teaspoons anise extract
2 teaspoons finely grated lemon zest
¾ cup (1½ sticks) unsalted butter, melted
and cooled

❄ DIRECTIONS

1. Whisk flour, baking powder, and salt together in a small bowl.

2. In a large bowl with an electric mixer on high speed, beat eggs until creamy, about 2 minutes. Add sugar gradually, beating until light and fluffy, about 3 minutes; beat in anise extract and lemon zest. Gradually beat in butter until thoroughly combined. Add about one-third of flour mixture and mix on low speed. Gradually add remaining flour, mixing just until blended.

3. Preheat *pizzelle* maker according to manufacturer's instructions.

Drop 2 tablespoons batter per *pizzelle* on griddle and cook until just turning an even golden brown, about 2 minutes. Remove carefully with fingertips or edge of an icing spatula and place directly on rack to cool completely. Alternatively, cut into quarters while still warm.

GOOD COOKIE TIP

Different pizzelle irons will have different designs and different size cookies, so you must use your judgment when spooning batter onto the hot griddle. It's kind of like making waffles—you feel your way through it in terms of amount of batter and cooking time. You can also flavor these with grated orange zest, which is a nice change. I have also made these flavored with spices such as ginger, cardamom, and cinnamon. Feel free to play around.

Powdered Walnut Cookies
Polvorones de Nuez

❋ **TYPE** *Shaped cookie*   ❋ **HABITAT** *Mexico*

❋ **DESCRIPTION** *This is a buttery, domed nut cookie (in this case made with walnuts) generously rolled in confectioners' sugar. These are a snap to make in the food processor.*

❋ **FIELD NOTES** *Round, crumbly sugar cookies with nuts in the dough appear in many cuisines, such as the Vanilla Crescents of Hungary (page 164), Pecan Butter Balls (page 112) from the southeastern United States, and Mexican wedding cakes, which aren't in the book, though they are virtually identical to the butter balls.*

❋ **LIFESPAN** *2 weeks at room temperature in airtight container in single layers separated by waxed paper*

Yield: *32 cookies*

❊ INGREDIENTS

¾ cup walnut halves
1¼ cups confectioners' sugar
¼ teaspoon salt

½ cup (1 stick) unsalted butter, cut into
tablespoons
½ teaspoon vanilla extract
1 cup all-purpose flour

❊ DIRECTIONS

1. Place walnuts, ¼ cup confectioners' sugar, and salt in a food processor, pulse to break up nuts, then process until nuts are finely ground. Add butter a few pieces at a time, pulsing to incorporate, then process until mixture is smooth; pulse in vanilla. Add flour and pulse until incorporated. Process until dough begins to form a ball. Place dough on large piece of plastic wrap, form into a very flat disc, cover completely with wrap, and refrigerate until firm enough to roll into balls, at least 2 hours or overnight.

2. Preheat oven to 350 degrees F. Line 2 rimmed cookie sheets with parchment paper.

3. Roll dough between your lightly floured palms into 1-inch balls and place 2 inches apart on cookie sheets. Gently flatten just enough so they don't roll off.

4. Bake until light golden brown around edges, about 15 minutes. Place pan on rack to cool for 5 minutes, then sift remaining 1 cup confectioners' sugar over warm cookies. After cookies have cooled completely, roll them in sugar on the sheets to cover completely.

Prune Stars · *Joulutortut*

❄ **TYPE** *Filled cookie*   ❄ **HABITAT** *Finland*

❄ **DESCRIPTION** *This prune-filled pastry, which hails from Beatrice Ojakangas* (The Great Scandinavian Baking Book), *is absolutely amazing. It begins with whipped heavy cream for the pastry—what's not to love?*

❄ **FIELD NOTES** *These delicacies are more of a pastry than a cookie, but they are a traditional Finnish Christmas treat and will add shape, texture, and flavor to your cookie tray.*

❄ **LIFESPAN** *Best the day they are made, but may be frozen in airtight container up to 1 month in single layers separated by waxed paper; reheat in 300-degree F oven until warmed through before serving*

Yield: *72 pastries*

❊ INGREDIENTS

Filling:
6 ounces pitted dried plums (prunes)
¾ cup water
½ teaspoon fresh lemon juice

Pastry:
3 cups all-purpose flour
1 teaspoon baking powder

¼ teaspoon salt
1½ cups heavy cream
1 cup (2 sticks) unsalted butter, softened

Topping:
1 large egg
1 tablespoon milk
Pearl sugar

❊ DIRECTIONS

1. To make filling, combine prunes and water in a medium saucepan and bring to a boil. Reduce heat to medium-low and simmer, stirring occasionally, until prunes are tender and liquid has evaporated by about half, about 10 minutes. Let cool slightly, place in food processor, and process until smooth. Pulse in lemon juice. Mixture should be thick enough to hold a shape when dropped from a spoon. If too thin, scrape back into saucepan and cook over medium-low heat until thickened, stirring constantly. Let cool to room temperature before using. (May be refrigerated in airtight container up to 1 week.)

2. To make pastry, whisk flour, baking powder, and salt together in a small bowl. In a large bowl with an electric mixer on medium-high speed, whip heavy cream until soft peaks form. Add flour gradually, beating on low speed until moist clumps form. Beat in butter until a soft dough forms. Scrape dough onto large piece of plastic wrap. Use wrap to help shape into 2 large, flat discs, then cover each completely with wrap. Refrigerate until firm enough to roll out, at least 2 hours or overnight.

3. Preheat oven to 400 degrees F. Line 2 cookie sheets with parchment paper.

4. Roll each piece of dough out to ¼-inch thickness on a lightly floured surface to a large rectangle about 18 x 24 inches. Fold each into thirds like a business letter, then roll and fold again the same way. Now roll out to an 18-inch square. Cut into 3-inch squares using a pizza cutter or sharp knife. Make 1½-inch-long slits on all four corners of each square, angling in toward the center as you would do if you were making a pinwheel. Place ½ teaspoon filling in center of each square. To form stars, fold every other corner in toward the center, pressing gently as you go to help pastry adhere (see photograph). Place pastries 2 inches apart on cookie sheets.

For topping, whisk egg and milk together until foamy. Brush each pastry with egg wash and sprinkle with pearl sugar, taking care not to get too much of either on cookie sheet.

5. Bake until light golden brown all over, about 20 minutes. Slide parchment onto racks to cool pastries completely.

Pumpkin Ginger Pillows

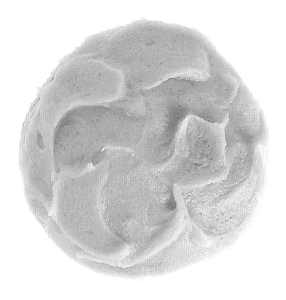

❄ **TYPE** *Drop cookie*   ❄ **HABITAT** *United States*

❄ **DESCRIPTION** *These are soft-as-a-pillow pumpkin-flavored cookies that also have a subtle crunch provided by pecans and chopped crystallized ginger. Once cooled, they are iced with a creamy brown-sugar frosting.*

❄ **FIELD NOTES** *Pumpkins were harvested by Native Americans and they, in turn, introduced the vegetable to the colonists, so pumpkins have been with us for a very long time. Some early recipes featured pumpkins hollowed out and filled with milk, spices, and sweetener to make a type of pumpkin pudding. While it might occur to you to cook your own pumpkin for the puree, don't bother. Canned pumpkin puree is a fine convenient product with no additives; it also has a silky texture that is nearly impossible to duplicate at home.*

❄ **LIFESPAN** *Unfrosted, 1 week at room temperature in airtight container*

Yield: *65 cookies*

❄ INGREDIENTS

Cookies:

2½ cups all-purpose flour
½ teaspoon salt
½ teaspoon baking powder
½ teaspoon baking soda
1 cup pecan halves, finely chopped
½ cup (3 ounces) finely chopped
   crystallized ginger
½ cup (1 stick) unsalted butter, softened
1½ cups firmly packed light brown sugar
1 teaspoon ground cinnamon
½ teaspoon ground ginger
¼ teaspoon ground cloves
¼ teaspoon freshly grated nutmeg
2 large eggs
One 15-ounce can (1¾ cups) pumpkin
   puree

Frosting:

2 tablespoons unsalted butter
¼ cup firmly packed light brown sugar
2 tablespoons heavy cream
1 cup confectioners' sugar, sifted

❄ DIRECTIONS

1. Preheat oven to 350 degrees F. Line 2 cookie sheets with parchment paper.

2. Whisk flour, salt, baking powder, and baking soda together in a medium bowl; stir in nuts and crystallized ginger.

3. In a large bowl with an electric mixer on medium-high speed, beat butter until creamy, about 2 minutes. Add brown sugar gradually, beating until light and fluffy, about 3 minutes. Beat in spices. Add eggs one at a time, beating well after each. Beat in pumpkin puree. Mixture might look curdled; that's okay. Add about one-third of flour mixture and mix on low speed. Gradually add remaining flour, mixing just until blended. Drop by generously rounded tablespoon 2 inches apart on cookie sheets.

4. Bake until light golden brown and just dry to touch, but still a little soft inside, about 15 minutes. You should be able to gently lift edge of a cookie up from sheet with a spatula, and a toothpick will test clean. Slide parchment onto racks to cool cookies completely.

5. To make frosting, combine butter and brown sugar in a small saucepan over medium heat, stirring occasionally, until butter melts. Bring to a boil and let boil 1 minute. Scrape mixture into a medium bowl and allow to cool 5 minutes. Add heavy cream and whip with electric mixer on medium-high speed until combined. Add confectioners' sugar and beat on medium speed until thick, creamy, and spreadable. Right before serving, spread frosting on each cookie using a small offset spatula.

Raisin Nut Cups

❄ **TYPE** *Filled cookie*   ❄ **HABITAT** *United States*

❄ **DESCRIPTION** *These pastry-like cookies are formed in mini-muffin tins. A rich cream cheese dough is formed in the shape of a cup, then filled with a buttery-sugary mixture of pecans and raisins.*

❄ **FIELD NOTES** *These tiny tarts are courtesy of my friend Chris Rivers's southern grandmother. The pecans, as well as the small tart shape, make them a typical southern sweet.*

❄ **LIFESPAN** *1 week at room temperature in airtight container*

Yield: *48 cookies*

❋ INGREDIENTS

Cream cheese dough:
1½ cups all-purpose flour
4 ounces (½ of an 8-ounce package) cold cream cheese, cut into tablespoon-sized pieces
½ cup (1 stick) cold unsalted butter, cut into tablespoons

Filling:
2 large eggs, separated
½ cup (1 stick) unsalted butter, softened
1 cup granulated sugar
1 teaspoon vanilla extract
1 cup pecan halves, finely chopped
1 cup dark raisins, chopped
Confectioners' sugar (optional)

❋ DIRECTIONS

1. Pulse flour in food processor. With machine on, add cream cheese and butter a few pieces at a time through feed tube and process until evenly combined and dough begins to form moist clumps. Cover with plastic wrap and refrigerate at least 1 hour or up to 2 days.

2. In a small, clean, grease-free bowl with an electric mixer on medium-high speed, whip egg whites until soft peaks form. In a medium bowl, beat butter on medium-high speed until creamy, about 3 minutes. Add granulated sugar gradually, beating until light and fluffy, about 5 minutes; beat in vanilla. Add egg yolks one at a time, beating well after each. Fold in whipped egg whites, pecans, and raisins until combined.

3. Preheat oven to 375 degrees F. Coat four 12-cup mini-muffin tins with non-stick spray.

4. Roll dough out to ¼-inch thickness on a lightly floured surface. Cut out circles with a 2½-inch round cookie cutter (fluted or straight edged), press a round into each muffin well, and smooth out the bottom and sides. Fill with about 1 teaspoon filling—it should come about three-quarters of the way up the sides; do not overfill.

5. Bake until light golden brown all over the top and slightly darker brown around edges, about 18 minutes. Place muffin tins on racks for a couple of minutes. To remove from pans, insert tip of sharp knife along edge of each tart and gently apply inward and upward pressure to release. Place tarts directly on racks to cool completely. Dust tops with confectioners' sugar right before serving, if desired.

Red Wine Raisin-Filled Cookies
Sfogliatelli Dolci

✳ **TYPE** *Filled cookie*   ✳ **HABITAT** *Italy*

✳ **DESCRIPTION** *This unusual pastry uses red wine and olive oil in the dough and is extremely easy to work with. It ends up as a log filled with spiced raisins and walnuts and a bit of currant jelly. After baking, the log is sliced crosswise into several pieces, giving you many cookies for not too much work.*

✳ **FIELD NOTES** *Valerie Cimino, managing editor at The Harvard Common Press, comes from an Italian family in which Christmas cookies are varied and plentiful. This is an old family recipe of hers, which she generously shared.*

✳ **LIFESPAN** *2 days at room temperature in airtight container*

Yield: *64 cookies*

❄ INGREDIENTS

Dough:
3½ to 4 cups all-purpose flour, as needed
½ cup light olive oil
½ cup red wine
½ cup water

Filling:
2⅔ cups dark raisins
1 cup walnut halves, chopped same size as raisins

2 tablespoons plus 2 teaspoons granulated sugar
1 teaspoon ground cinnamon
½ cup red currant jelly

Topping:
3 tablespoons granulated sugar
1 teaspoon ground cinnamon
Light olive oil

❄ DIRECTIONS

1. Preheat oven to 325 degrees F. Line 2 cookie sheets with parchment paper.

2. Whisk flour in a small bowl.

3. Combine olive oil, wine, and water in a large bowl. Add 3½ cups of the flour and mix on low speed with an electric mixer just until blended. You should have a soft but not sticky dough. Add any portion of remaining flour if dough is too sticky.

4. Toss together filling ingredients in a medium bowl until combined. Stir sugar and cinnamon for topping together in a small bowl.

5. Divide dough into 4 pieces and roll each piece out to a 6 x 16-inch rectangle on a lightly floured surface. Have dough horizontal on work surface. Spread each piece of dough with 2 tablespoons jelly, leaving a 1-inch border of naked dough all around.

Sprinkle one-quarter of filling over jelly, leaving a 1-inch border of jelly all around the filling. Fold long top half of dough down over the filling, almost completely encasing it; fold bottom half up over the pastry. Pinch seam gently, but well. Pick up log and place seam side down on cookie sheet; tuck ends underneath. Brush top lightly with olive oil and sprinkle generously with cinnamon sugar. Repeat with remaining dough, filling, and topping. There will be 2 rolls per cookie sheet.

6. Bake just until light golden brown on bottom and dry to touch on top, about 32 minutes; do not overbake or pastry will toughen. Slide parchment onto racks to cool logs. Cut each log crosswise into 1-inch-thick pieces (about 16 per log). These are particularly delectable while still a bit warm.

Ribbon Cookies

✳ **TYPE** *Refrigerator cookie*   ✳ **HABITAT** *United States*

✳ **DESCRIPTION** *Ribbon candy is very popular at Christmastime, and these cookies have similar colorful stripes. I found a three-flavored cookie recipe in a* Southern Living *cookbook, but gave it some new flavors and twists. This version keeps very well, always a boon at the holidays.*

✳ **FIELD NOTES** *The ribbon candy that these cookies are based upon, while very American, has its roots in France and Italy, where confectioners have been pulling sugar at least since the Renaissance.*

✳ **LIFESPAN** *1 month at room temperature in airtight container*

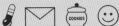

Yield: *100 cookies*

❄ INGREDIENTS

2½ cups all-purpose flour
½ teaspoon salt
1½ teaspoons baking powder
1 cup (2 sticks) unsalted butter, softened
1½ cups granulated sugar
1 teaspoon vanilla extract
1 large egg
¼ cup minced candied cherries

¼ cup finely chopped unsalted natural pistachios
2 drops green liquid food coloring (optional)
½ ounce unsweetened chocolate, melted
¼ cup miniature semisweet chocolate chips

❄ DIRECTIONS

1. Line bottom and sides of a 4 x 8-inch straight-sided loaf pan with plastic wrap, using enough to overhang all sides.

2. Whisk flour, salt, and baking powder together in a small bowl.

3. In a large bowl with an electric mixer on medium-high speed, beat butter until creamy, about 2 minutes. Add sugar gradually, beating until light and fluffy, about 3 minutes; beat in vanilla. Beat in egg. Add about one-third of flour mixture and mix on low speed. Gradually add remaining flour, mixing just until blended. Divide dough into three equal parts and place in individual bowls. Add cherries to one, stir until combined, and pat in an even layer in loaf pan. Add pistachios to another, stir until combined, and stir in food coloring, if using. Pat into an even layer on top of cherry layer. Stir melted chocolate and chocolate morsels into the third until well blended, and pat in an even layer on top of pistachio layer. Fold plastic wrap over dough to cover completely and refrigerate until firm enough to slice, at least 4 hours or overnight.

4. Preheat oven to 375 degrees F. Line 2 cookie sheets with parchment paper.

5. Unwrap loaf pan and unmold cookie dough by pulling up on plastic wrap to aid the process. Peel plastic completely away. Cut ⅓-inch-thick slices crosswise off end of loaf. Lay slices flat on work surface so that various layers of cookie are horizontal in front of you. Cut each cookie into 4 pieces, top to bottom, so that each slice has all 3 flavors. Place 2 inches apart on cookie sheets. Bake just until light golden brown, about 10 minutes. Slide parchment onto racks to cool cookies completely.

Salt-Dough Ornament Cookies

✳ **TYPE** *Rolled cookie*   ✳ **HABITAT** *United States*

✳ **DESCRIPTION** *These are inedible cookies, but the salt-and-flour dough is so easy to work with and there is such an endless possibility for the decoration that I had to include them. After these rolled cookies have cooled, you can paint them with acrylic paints and even decorate them with glitter and sequins — whatever you like! You can make a children's party out of it with baking taking place ahead of time and the decorating as the party project.*

✳ **FIELD NOTES** *Every kindergarten and elementary school seems to have at least one teacher who knows how to make these. There are also many versions floating around the Internet, and they are all basically the same. Where they originated, who knows?*

✳ **LIFESPAN** *Forever*

Yield: *twenty-five 3-inch cookie ornaments*

❋ INGREDIENTS

Cookies:

4 cups all-purpose flour
1 cup salt
1⅓ cups water, at room temperature

Decoration:

Acrylic paints, paintbrushes, glitter, sequins, spray varnish, etc.
8⅓ yards ⅛- to ¼-inch ribbon, cut into 12-inch lengths

❋ DIRECTIONS

1. Preheat oven to 250 degrees F. Line 2 cookie sheets with parchment paper.

2. Combine flour and salt in a large bowl. With an electric mixer on medium speed, gradually add water, beating until moist clumps form. Dough may not form a ball; that's okay. Remove to a work surface and knead for a minute or two until it comes together and smooths out. Roll dough out to ¼-inch thickness on lightly floured surface and cut out shapes of your choice; insert end of a chopstick in top of each ornament and swirl around until a hole is formed. You can also use a drinking straw. Place on cookie sheets.

3. Bake for 55 minutes, flip cookies over, and bake for another 55 minutes. Cookies should be dry and hard, but not colored. Slide parchment onto racks to cool cookies completely. Paint, decorate, and allow to dry. Spray with varnish, if desired. Thread ribbon through hole and knot about 1 inch from the ends. They are now ready to hang.

GOOD COOKIE TIP

I tried to bake these at a higher temperature to lessen the baking time, but it just doesn't work as well. The cookies puff, warp, and color, so plan to make these when you'll be around the house for a while.

Scandinavian Sand Cookies
Kanelkakor

✳ **TYPE** *Shaped cookie*   ✳ **HABITAT** *Sweden*

✳ **DESCRIPTION** *These simple sugar cookies are made extra rich with an additional egg yolk. They feature cardamom, a highly aromatic spice, in both the dough and the sugar-spice topping.*

✳ **FIELD NOTES** *Cardamom is a very popular spice in Scandinavia, where it is used in both desserts and savory dishes.*

✳ **LIFESPAN** *2 weeks at room temperature in airtight container*

Yield: *65 cookies*

❄ INGREDIENTS

Cookies:
2 cups all-purpose flour
1 teaspoon baking powder
¾ cup (1½ sticks) unsalted butter, softened
1¼ cups granulated sugar
1 teaspoon ground cardamom
1 teaspoon ground cinnamon

1 large egg
1 large egg yolk

Topping:
1 large egg
¼ cup granulated sugar
¼ teaspoon ground cardamom
¼ teaspoon ground cinnamon

❄ DIRECTIONS

1. Whisk flour and baking powder together in a small bowl.

2. In a large bowl with an electric mixer on medium-high speed, beat butter until creamy, about 2 minutes. Add sugar gradually and beat until light and fluffy, about 3 minutes. Beat in cardamom and cinnamon, then beat in whole egg and egg yolk. Add about one-third of flour mixture and mix on low speed. Gradually add remaining flour, mixing just until blended. Scrape dough onto large piece of plastic wrap. Use wrap to help shape it into a large, flat disc, then cover completely with wrap. Refrigerate until firm enough to roll into balls, at least 1 hour or overnight.

3. Preheat oven to 350 degrees F. Line 2 cookie sheets with parchment paper. To make topping, whisk egg in a small bowl. In a separate bowl, stir together sugar, cardamom, and cinnamon.

4. Roll dough between your palms into 1-inch balls. Dip "top" of balls in egg, then sugar mixture, and place 2 inches apart on cookie sheets, sugar side up. Bake until light golden brown around edges and topping is slightly crackled looking, about 17 minutes. Slide parchment onto racks to cool cookies completely.

Sherried Mini Fruitcakes

❄ **TYPE** *Molded cookie*   ❄ **HABITAT** *England*

❄ **DESCRIPTION** *Some people like fruitcake, and some do not, but there is no denying that fruitcake shouts Christmas. This recipe uses high-quality candied and dried fruits, which makes it particularly flavorful—give it a try! You can order the candied fruit mixture from King Arthur Flour The Baker's Catalogue (see Resources), or look in your local specialty food store. The mixtures from the supermarket are usually dry and have poor flavor.*

❄ **FIELD NOTES** *While fruitcake has become the butt of jokes in the United States, it is held in high esteem in England.*

❄ **LIFESPAN** *2 months at room temperature in airtight container*

Yield: *45 cakes*

❄ INGREDIENTS

½ pound (1⅓ cups) mixed diced candied fruit, such as citron, pineapple, citrus peels, and cherries

¼ pound dried Calimyrna figs (about 6), stemmed and minced

¼ pound pitted Medjool dates (about 8), minced

¼ pound (⅓ cup) dark raisins

¼ pound (⅓ cup) golden raisins

¼ cup honey

¼ cup dry sherry, plus more for soaking

1 cup all-purpose flour

Pinch of baking soda

1 cup pecan halves, finely chopped

½ cup (1 stick) unsalted butter, softened

⅔ cup granulated sugar

½ teaspoon ground cinnamon

2 large eggs

❄ DIRECTIONS

1. Place candied and dried fruit in a large bowl and toss to combine. Add honey and sherry, stir well, cover bowl with plastic wrap, and let sit at room temperature overnight to macerate or, alternatively, microwave on high power for 2 minutes; stir and let cool.

2. Preheat oven to 325 degrees F. Coat four 12-cup mini-muffin tins with non-stick spray.

3. Stir together flour and baking soda in a small bowl. Stir in nuts.

4. In a large bowl with an electric mixer on medium-high speed, beat butter until creamy, about 2 minutes. Add sugar gradually, beating until light and fluffy, about 3 minutes; beat in cinnamon. Add eggs one at a time, beating well after each. Add about one-third of flour mixture and mix on low speed. Gradually add remaining flour, mixing just until blended. Fold in fruit mixture. Place a generously rounded tablespoon of batter in each muffin well.

5. Bake until light golden brown and a toothpick inserted in center comes out clean, about 25 minutes. Cool muffin tins on racks a couple of minutes, then carefully invert and transfer cakes to racks to cool completely. Place in a single layer in a cookie tin, pierce each with a skewer several times, and generously sprinkle with sherry to moisten. Cover with a piece of parchment paper or aluminum foil and make another single layer of cakes if tin is deep enough. Just make sure all of them are well moistened with sherry. Seal the tins and let sit overnight. Sprinkle with sherry again and reseal the tins. Repeat the following day and the next. These are best eaten at least 1 week after baking and after receiving at least 4 doses of sherry. If storing longer, add more sherry about every 3 days.

Shortbread Fans

✳ **TYPE** *Rolled cookie*   ✳ **HABITAT** *Scotland*

✳ **DESCRIPTION** *This is the butteriest butter cookie of them all. A whopping 1 pound of butter is packed in this cookie, with a supporting cast of sugar, flour, and vanilla. There are versions that do not even include vanilla, as some bakers like the natural sweetness of the butter to shine through; it's your choice—you can leave it out if you like. Shortbread is easy to make and stores well.*

✳ **FIELD NOTES** *The "short" in* shortbread *refers to the fact that the dough itself is very "short," that is, loaded with shortening, in this case, butter. The term* short *has been used at least since medieval times in Britain.*

✳ **LIFESPAN** *2 weeks at room temperature in airtight container*

Yield: *five 8-inch discs, each yielding 8 fans, for a total of 40 fans*

❄ INGREDIENTS

5 cups all-purpose flour, sifted
2 cups (4 sticks) unsalted butter, softened

1 cup granulated sugar
1 teaspoon vanilla extract (optional)

❄ DIRECTIONS

1. Line 3 cookie sheets with parchment paper and sprinkle lightly with flour.

2. Whisk flour in a medium bowl.

3. In a large bowl with an electric mixer on medium-high speed, beat butter until creamy, about 3 minutes. Add sugar gradually and beat on high speed until very light and fluffy. This may take as long as 8 minutes. Do not rush; mixture should be almost white in color. Beat in vanilla, if using. Add about one-third of flour and mix on low speed. Gradually add remaining flour, mixing just until blended.

4. Divide dough in half, shaping each into a flat disc. Roll out one disc directly onto cookie sheet to ¼-inch thickness. Gently place an 8-inch cake pan over dough and cut out two 8-inch circles, removing and saving any scraps. Repeat with the second disc, rolling out onto second cookie sheet and cutting two more circles. Take scraps and roll out on last cookie sheet, cutting out a fifth circle. Crimp edges, like you would a piecrust, to create a scalloped effect. Or use round bottom end of a decorator tip to cut out half-moon shapes all around edges. Score 8 wedges into surface of dough using a small sharp knife. Prick shortbread all over with a fork or skewer either randomly or decoratively. Refrigerate for 1 hour or overnight, if desired.

5. Preheat oven to 325 degrees F. Bake just until edges turn very light golden brown, but top of shortbread should remain as white as possible, about 30 minutes. Immediately cut into wedges along score lines while shortbread is still warm. This is best accomplished with a knife that is longer than width of shortbread; hold knife above round and cut, pressing knife straight down, instead of dragging tip through. Cool on sheets on racks for a couple of minutes, then carefully transfer wedges to racks to cool completely.

Sicilian White Cookies
Pastine Bianche

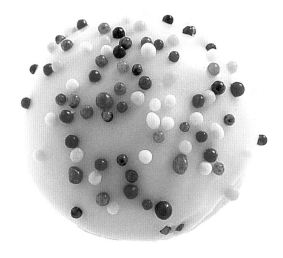

❄ **TYPE** *Shaped cookie*   ❄ **HABITAT** *Italy*

❄ **DESCRIPTION** *These soft, tender, cakey cookies are generously flavored with anise, lemon, and vanilla. Their domed shape is crowned with an opaque white glaze and sprinkling of tiny multicolored nonpareil candies. These look and taste festive.*

❄ **FIELD NOTES** *This is another recipe given to me by Valerie Cimino, who says her mom makes them every holiday season. Her mom's recipe was for twice the amount, and the directions said that it made "a lot." It certainly did; even cut in half, as it is here, you will have a generous amount (feel free to double it, though, if you like; the recipe doubles perfectly). The only change I made from the original was to replace lemon extract with lemon zest, which I prefer.*

❄ **LIFESPAN** *2 weeks at room temperature in airtight container stored in a single layer*

Yield: *60 cookies*

❄ INGREDIENTS

Cookies:
2½ cups all-purpose flour
1 tablespoon plus 1½ teaspoons baking powder
½ cup (1 stick) unsalted butter, softened
½ cup granulated sugar
2 teaspoons finely grated lemon zest
½ teaspoon anise extract
½ teaspoon vanilla extract

2 large eggs
¼ cup milk

Glaze:
2 cups confectioners' sugar, sifted
¼ teaspoon cream of tartar
¼ cup milk

Multicolored nonpareils

❄ DIRECTIONS

1. Preheat oven to 350 degrees F. Line 2 cookie sheets with parchment paper.

2. Whisk flour and baking powder together in a small bowl.

3. In a large bowl with an electric mixer on medium-high speed, beat butter until creamy, about 2 minutes. Add granulated sugar gradually, beating until light and fluffy, about 3 minutes; beat in lemon zest and extracts. Add eggs one at a time, beating well after each. Add about one-third of flour and mix on low speed. Gradually add milk and remaining flour, mixing just until blended. Mixture should stiffen but still be a bit sticky. Roll dough into 1-inch balls between your floured palms and place 2 inches apart on cookie sheets.

4. To make glaze, whisk together confectioners' sugar and cream of tartar in a small bowl. Whisk in milk gradually until you have a thick but fluid icing (you might need more or less of the milk).

5. Bake just until light golden brown on bottom, about 10 minutes; tops will be white, dry, soft, and springy to touch. Slide parchment onto racks.

Immediately pick up each cookie and dip top half into glaze; allow excess to drip back into bowl. Set cookie, icing side up, back on parchment on rack; immediately sprinkle with nonpareils while icing is wet. Work quickly so that you are dipping still-warm cookies into glaze and nonpareils are sticking to still-wet icing. Allow to cool and dry completely.

Snickerdoodles

❄ **TYPE** *Shaped cookie*   ❄ **HABITAT** *United States*

❄ **DESCRIPTION** *This is a deceptively simple sugar cookie recipe. The ingredients are quite basic—butter, sugar, cinnamon—but the result is more than a sum of its parts; these cookies come together just perfectly in terms of balancing ease of preparation, common ingredients, crunch, and flavor. They are so simple, I didn't think my kids would like them, but then one twin determined them to be his favorite cookie in the book.*

❄ **FIELD NOTES** *These hail from New England, with versions dating from the mid- to late 1800s. The name's origin, however, is a bit more elusive. Some food historians say it is just a made-up nonsense word that seems to appeal to kids and adults alike.*

❄ **LIFESPAN** *2 weeks at room temperature in airtight container*

Yield: *60 cookies*

❄ INGREDIENTS

Cookies:
 2¾ cups all-purpose flour
 2 teaspoons cream of tartar
 1 teaspoon baking soda
 ½ teaspoon salt
 1 cup (2 sticks) unsalted butter, softened

 1½ cups granulated sugar
 2 large eggs

Topping:
 ¼ cup granulated sugar
 2 teaspoons ground cinnamon

❄ DIRECTIONS

1. Whisk flour, cream of tartar, baking soda, and salt together in a small bowl.

2. In a large bowl with an electric mixer on medium-high speed, beat butter until creamy, about 2 minutes. Add sugar gradually, beating until light and fluffy, about 3 minutes. Add eggs one at a time, beating well after each. Add about one-third of flour mixture and mix on low speed. Gradually add remaining flour, mixing just until blended. Cover with plastic wrap and refrigerate until firm enough to roll into balls, at least 2 hours or overnight.

3. Preheat oven to 375 degrees F. Line 2 cookie sheets with parchment paper.

 To make topping, combine sugar and cinnamon in a small bowl.

4. Roll dough into 1-inch balls between your palms, then roll in cinnamon sugar to coat. Place 2 inches apart on cookie sheets; gently flatten just enough so they don't roll off. Bake just until light golden brown around edges, about 12 minutes. Slide parchment onto racks to cool cookies completely.

Springerle

❄ **TYPE** *Molded cookie*   ❄ **HABITAT** *Germany*

❄ **DESCRIPTION** *You will need special springerle molds to make these pale anise-flavored cookies (see Resources). Springerle are very hard, dry cookies, which, to my mind, are more decorative than palatable. The finely textured dough displays the raised scenes from the molds, which can then be painted with edible gold or silver, if you like. The yield will vary greatly depending on the size and depth of your molds. The following recipe is based upon one that dates back at least 400 years; I have tried to find a balance between a recipe that works easily in the molds and one that it is good to eat. Aging the cookies helps their palatability.*

❄ **FIELD NOTES** *Historians believe that cookie-like pastries imprinted by molds date back to pagan celebrations. Animal sacrifices were common, but the poor, unable to spare any live animals, offered baked goods featuring animal shapes instead. The word* springerle *derives from the word describing a leaping action, and leaping horses happen to be a very popular design in springerle molds even today.*

❄ **LIFESPAN** *3 months at room temperature in airtight container; for eating, texture improves if allowed to sit for at least 1 week*

Yield: *about twenty 3-inch cookies*

❊ INGREDIENTS

Cookies:
7 cups cake flour, sifted
3 large eggs, at room temperature
3 cups confectioners' sugar, sifted
¼ cup (½ stick) unsalted butter, softened
1 teaspoon anise extract
2 teaspoons finely grated lemon zest
(optional)

1 tablespoon milk
¼ teaspoon baking powder
Crushed anise seeds (optional)

Decoration (optional):
Edible gold and silver powder
Vodka
Soft artist's brush

❊ DIRECTIONS

1. Line 2 cookie sheets with parchment paper.

2. Whisk flour in a large bowl.

3. In another large bowl with an electric mixer on high speed, whip eggs and confectioners' sugar together until very light and fluffy, about 5 minutes. Beat in butter, anise extract, and lemon zest, if using. Combine milk and baking powder, then beat into egg mixture. Gradually add 6 cups flour, beating on low speed until combined; mixture should be somewhat dry and crumbly, but should hold together if squeezed. Add more flour if needed.

4. Roll out dough to ¼- to ⅓-inch thickness (depending on depth of molds) on floured surface lightly sprinkled with crushed anise seeds, if using. Lightly flour springerle molds or springerle rolling pin and make impressions in dough. If using single molds, press firmly into dough, remove mold, and cut around edge of mold (usually a circle or square shape) to create individual cookie. If using a multiple mold, cut individual cookies apart after creating impressions.

If using rolling pin, roll over dough once using slow, even pressure; cut individual cookies apart. Place cookies 2 inches apart on cookie sheets and let sit, uncovered, overnight at room temperature.

5. Preheat oven to 300 degrees F. Bake until dry to touch, about 20 minutes. Tops of cookies should remain as white as possible, but bottoms will just be starting to color. Slide parchment onto racks to cool cookies completely.

6. To make optional decoration, place a small amount of gold or silver powder in a small bowl and add vodka, a few drops at a time, until a thick paint consistency is reached. Paint raised impressions on cookies with the paint. Allow to dry and store.

GOOD COOKIE TIP
Some springerle bakers say that flouring the molds will obscure the designs. Instead, they suggest coating them with nonstick spray. Try a variety of approaches to see what works best with your dough and your molds.

Spritz Cookies

❋ **TYPE** *Pressed cookie*   ❋ **HABITAT** *Germany*

❋ **DESCRIPTION** *These have a crispy, buttery texture and delicate almond-vanilla flavor. You can form them with a spritz cookie press or you can use a pastry bag fitted with a large open-star tip (such as an Ateco #824 or #844). Your butter has to be very soft for the recipe to work. If the dough is too stiff (from cold butter), it will be hard to press. With the spritz maker, you can easily make many different shapes by changing the disc in the machine; most models come with at least a dozen different ones. Take a look at my suggested variations (Related Species), as one is as delicious as the next.*

❋ **FIELD NOTES** *The word* spritzen *means "to squirt or spurt" in German, and whether you are using a spritz cookie press or a pastry bag and tip, the action is indeed that of squirting the dough out of the mechanism. These cookies are popular in Scandinavia, as well.*

❋ **RELATED SPECIES** Gussied-Up Spritz: *Before baking, press a candied cherry half or whole almond in center of each cookie or sprinkle with granulated or colored sugar;* Spritz Sandwiches: *After baking, sandwich two identical shapes together with melted chocolate or lemon curd. Allow filling to extend beyond edges a little bit, then roll in finely chopped nuts, if desired;* Apricot-Pistachio Spritz Sandwiches: *Sandwich two* *together with apricot jam and roll edges in pistachios;* Chocolate-Raspberry Spritz Sandwiches: *Sandwich two together with raspberry jam, then dip half in dark chocolate and cover with chocolate sprinkles;* Peppermint and White Chocolate Spritz: *Dip half of the cookie in melted white chocolate and sprinkle with crushed red-and-white peppermint candies;* Classic American Butter Cookies: *Omit the almond extract and increase the vanilla extract to 1½ teaspoons.*

❄ **LIFESPAN** *2 weeks at room temperature in airtight container*

Yield: *50 cookies*

❄ INGREDIENTS

2½ cups all-purpose flour
¼ teaspoon salt
1 cup (2 sticks) unsalted butter, softened
½ cup granulated sugar

½ cup confectioners' sugar
1 teaspoon almond extract
1 teaspoon vanilla extract
1 large egg

❄ DIRECTIONS

1. Preheat oven to 375 degrees F. Line 2 cookie sheets with parchment paper.

2. Whisk flour and salt together in a small bowl.

3. In a large bowl with an electric mixer on medium-high speed, beat butter until creamy, about 2 minutes. Add both sugars gradually, beating until light and fluffy, about 3 minutes; beat in extracts. Beat in egg. Mixture should be very light and smooth at this point. Add about one-third of flour mixture and mix on low speed. Gradually add remaining flour, mixing just until blended.

4. Following manufacturer's instructions for your spritz cookie maker, assemble machine with disc of choice. Press out cookies 2 inches apart directly onto cookie sheets. If using a pastry bag and star tip, just scrape dough into bag and press out rosette-shaped cookies directly onto sheet.

5. Bake just until light golden brown around edges, about 10 minutes. Slide parchment onto racks to cool cookies completely.

Sugar Cookies, Classic Rolled

❄ **TYPE** *Rolled cookies*　　❄ **HABITAT** *United States*

❄ **DESCRIPTION** *Here is a basic recipe for buttery, crisp sugar cookies. While it is simple, it is equally tasty. This variation uses colored sugars to decorate the tops. The four recipes that follow use the same cookie dough, but are formed and decorated to give you very different results.*

❄ **FIELD NOTES** *This is often the first rolled cookie taught to American children. Recipes from the early 1800s are very similar in that none of them use baking powder, which didn't come into use till decades later. The lack of leavener helps keep the cookies flat, which yields a nice surface for whatever kind of decoration you like.*

❄ **LIFESPAN** *1 month at room temperature in an airtight container*

Yield: *thirty-six 3-inch cookies*

❄ INGREDIENTS

3¾ cups all-purpose flour
½ teaspoon salt
1½ cups (3 sticks) unsalted butter,
   softened

1½ cups granulated sugar
1½ teaspoons vanilla extract
3 large eggs
Colored sugars and granulated sugar

❄ DIRECTIONS

1. Whisk flour and salt together in a small bowl.

2. In large bowl with an electric mixer on medium-high speed, beat butter until creamy, about 2 minutes. Add granulated sugar gradually and beat until light and fluffy, about 3 minutes; beat in vanilla. Add eggs one at a time, beating well after each. Add about one-third of flour mixture and mix on low speed. Gradually add remaining flour, mixing just until blended. Scrape dough onto large piece of plastic wrap, form into 2 very flat discs, cover completely with wrap, and refrigerate until firm enough to roll out, at least 2 hours or overnight.

3. Preheat oven to 350 degrees F. Line 2 cookie sheets with parchment paper.

4. Take 1 disc and roll out to ¼-inch thickness on floured surface; you may need to flour the pin, too. Cut out cookies with shapes of choice. Place 2 inches apart on cookie sheet. Decorate with colored sugars or granulated sugar as you wish. Bake until edges just begin to turn light golden brown, about 10 minutes. Slide parchment onto racks to cool cookies completely.

GOOD COOKIE TIP

This dough is sensitive to heat and humidity; the more of each there is, the stickier the dough. If you find you have a soft, sticky dough after following the directions, just add a bit more flour and you will have success.

You will probably want to make cookies of all sizes and shapes. Just make sure that similarly sized cookies are on the same pan so that they bake evenly.

Sugar Cookies, Iced

❄ **TYPE** *Rolled cookies*   ❄ **HABITAT** *United States*

❄ **DESCRIPTION** *Here decoration is provided by royal icing, applied after the cookies have cooled. For a sparkle effect, sprinkle colored sugars on top of the wet icing. Or embed gold and silver dragées or red-hot candies in the wet icing.*

❄ **LIFESPAN** *1 month at room temperature in an airtight container in single layers separated by waxed paper*

Yield: *thirty-six 3-inch cookies*

❄ INGREDIENTS

1 recipe Classic Rolled Sugar Cookies
(page 148)

Thick royal icing (yields 1⅓ cups):
3¾ cups confectioners' sugar, sifted
3 large egg whites
Gel, paste, liquid, or powdered food
coloring (see Tip below)

Medium royal icing:
3¾ cups confectioners' sugar, sifted
3 large egg whites

1 tablespoon water
Gel, paste, liquid, or powdered food
coloring

Thin royal icing:
3¾ cups confectioners' sugar, sifted
3 large egg whites
2 tablespoons water
Gel, paste, liquid, or powdered food
coloring

❄ DIRECTIONS

1. Bake and cool the cookies as directed on page 149.

2. For each of the icings, place confectioners' sugar, egg whites, and water, if called for, in clean, grease-free bowls and whip with an electric mixer on high speed until thick and creamy, about 6 minutes. Tint, if desired, with food coloring (powdered colors are dusted over dry icing). Start with small amounts of gel, paste, or liquid color; you can always add more.

3. The thickest icing is used to pipe a complete border around the cookie's edge (to form a retaining wall). A dab of it will be stiff enough to hold a peak. Medium icing can be used to create three-dimensional effects on already-dry icing (like adding eyes to an already-iced cookie). A dab of it will puddle slightly and form a thick, dimensional circle. The thinnest icing is used to cover cookies completely, or to cover partial sections outlined with a thick textured border. Two colors (or more) of thin icing can be swirled together to create a marbled effect.

To ice cookies, scrape thick icing into a pastry bag fitted with coupler and very small round tip (such as Ateco #2) and pipe an outline, either around edge of cookie or to define a section you want to cover with icing. Make sure to create a solid line all the way around. Allow to dry, then fill outlined section with thin icing. Place thin icing in a pastry bag with very small round tip and allow it to flow within outlined area. This will yield a cookie completely covered with a smooth layer of icing, which will dry hard. To embellish with details, such as eyes, use medium icing on the dry cookie.

GOOD COOKIE TIP

Royal icing is made with raw egg whites. You can substitute powdered egg whites, available in any well-stocked supermarket in the baking aisle. Reconstitute according to manufacturer's instructions. You can occasionally find containers of pasteurized egg whites in the refrigerated dairy aisle.

Sugar Cookies, Painted

❄ **TYPE** *Rolled cookies*　　❄ **HABITAT** *United States*

❄ **DESCRIPTION** *Using my basic sugar cookie dough, you can also decorate them with edible "paint" as opposed to sugar or icing. Very easy to make, the paint is applied before baking, so you do not have to worry about raw eggs.*

❄ **LIFESPAN** *1 month at room temperature in an airtight container*

Yield: *thirty-six 3-inch cookies*

❄ **INGREDIENTS**

Edible paint:
　4 large egg yolks
　Gel, paste, or liquid food coloring

Soft artist's brush
Dough for 1 recipe Classic Rolled Sugar
　Cookies (page 148)

❄ **DIRECTIONS**

1. To make edible paint, place egg yolks in small bowl and whisk until loosened and smooth. Divide into as many small bowls as you want colors. Tint each batch to color of your choice, stirring in tiny bits of color at a time (you can always add more). Stir until color is well mixed with the yolk.

2. Roll out and cut cookies as directed. Use a soft paintbrush to paint cookies with edible paint as desired. Bake and cool as directed on page 149.

Sugar Cookies, Stained Glass

❄ **TYPE** *Rolled cookies*   ❄ **HABITAT** *United States*

❄ **DESCRIPTION** *Here you cut out small shapes from sugar cookies and fill in the space with crushed hard candies, which melt and make "stained glass." The trick is to finely and evenly crush the candies and to carefully fill in the spaces for a neat appearance.*

❄ **LIFESPAN** *1 month at room temperature in an airtight container in single layers separated by waxed paper*

Yield: *thirty-six 3-inch cookies*

❄ **INGREDIENTS**

Hard candies, such as LifeSavers, in various flavors and colors

Dough for 1 recipe Classic Rolled Sugar Cookies (page 148)

❄ **DIRECTIONS**

1. Prepare candies by placing like flavors and colors in a zipper-lock plastic bag and crushing into an even powder with a rolling pin.

2. Roll out and cut cookies as directed. Once on cookie sheets, cut smaller shapes out of centers of cookies and remove. Treat these small shapes as scraps and re-roll. You can even cut out several small shapes to create a multicolored, multishaped cookie. Fill each space with powdered candy. Do this very carefully, gently spooning it into the spaces, not allowing any to get on top of cookies. Fill spaces evenly and as completely as possible. A very small demitasse spoon is great for this.

3. Bake as directed on page 149, but cool cookies completely on sheets placed on racks.

Sugar Cookies, 3-D Ornament

❄ **TYPE** *Rolled cookies*   ❄ **HABITAT** *United States*

❄ **DESCRIPTION** *It is easy to create three-dimensional tree ornaments with sugar cookie dough. You simply make a few extra cuts before baking, then assemble using thick royal icing after they have cooled. Consider making one for each family member or guest.*

❄ **LIFESPAN** *At least 1 week out in the air or 2 weeks at room temperature in an airtight container in a single layer*

Yield: *eighteen 3-inch ornaments*

❄ INGREDIENTS

Dough for 1 recipe Classic Rolled Sugar
Cookies (page 148)
Thick Royal Icing (page 151)

Colored sugars, granulated sugar, gold and
silver *dragées,* and cinnamon red-hot
candies
10 yards ⅛-inch fabric ribbon, cut into
12-inch lengths

❄ DIRECTIONS

1. Roll out dough as directed on page 149. For this recipe, you want to choose large (3- to 4-inch) simple shapes, such as rounds, squares, diamonds, hearts, and ovals with straight or fluted edges. Cut out two of each shape; these will make one ornament. Once placed on cookie sheets, cut one of each shape straight down middle, but do not separate the halves. In the other whole cookie, insert end of a chopstick in top, slightly off center, and swirl around until a hole is formed. You can also use a drinking straw, if you have one on hand.

2. Bake as directed on page 149. Cut through the scored cookies as soon as they come out of the oven; keeping pairs together, transfer all cookies to rack to cool completely.

3. Scrape the icing into pastry bag fitted with coupler and very small round tip (such as Ateco #2) and pipe designs as desired, steering clear of the raw edges of the cut cookies and center of whole cookies (see photograph). Sprinkle with sugars and/or embellish with *dragées* and candies, if desired. Allow icing to dry.

4. To assemble ornaments, pipe icing onto raw cookie edges and affix to whole cookie of same shape, bisecting it perfectly. Prop up this cookie half with a small paper cup or wadded piece of parchment paper and allow to dry. Turn over and affix other cookie half to other side. Embellish with additional icing, if desired, and prop up appropriately. Allow to dry completely. Thread ribbon through hole and knot about 1 inch from ends. They are now ready to hang.

Sugarplums

✳ **TYPE** *Shaped confections*   ✳ **HABITAT** *United States and Portugal*

✳ **DESCRIPTION** *These are small candies made from a mélange of dried fruit and are great to make with kids, in which case, use the orange juice. Otherwise, for an adult version, go for the "spirited" variation. There are several ways to finish them off, and I suggest that you choose at least two of the options. The key to this recipe is to have the nuts and fruits all the same small size. You may chop them by hand or chop one by one in a food processor, pulsing until the desired size is reached.*

✳ **FIELD NOTES** *The original version may have originated in Portugal, where fresh black figs and cooked green plums were used to make a similar candy. I always associate them with the Sugarplum Fairies from* The Nutcracker *ballet. I think this is what the fairies eat when they want to sneak a sweet treat!*

✳ **LIFESPAN** *1 month refrigerated in airtight container*

Yield: *36 sugarplums*

❄ INGREDIENTS

¼ cup finely chopped dates
¼ cup finely chopped dried figs
¼ cup finely chopped pitted dried plums
  (prunes)
¼ cup finely chopped dried cherries
¼ cup finely chopped golden raisins
½ cup finely chopped pecans
¼ cup unsweetened grated coconut
  (available in health food stores)

2 tablespoons light or dark rum, orange
  liqueur, or orange juice
Granulated sugar

Toppings (optional):
Confectioners' sugar
Finely chopped almonds, hazelnuts, pecans,
  pistachios, or walnuts
Finely grated bittersweet chocolate
Unsweetened cocoa powder
Unsweetened grated coconut

❄ DIRECTIONS

1. Place all the dried fruit, pecans, coconut, and liquid of choice in a medium bowl. Mix together by hand until thoroughly combined; it should hold together when compressed. If it is dry, add a little more liquid.

2. Roll mixture into 1-inch balls between your palms, compressing mixture so that it sticks together. Place granulated sugar in a small bowl and roll sugarplums in it to coat completely; place in small fluted paper cups, if desired.

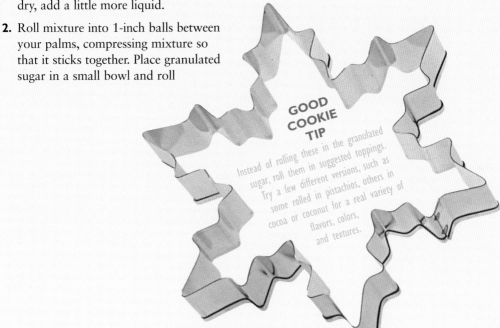

GOOD COOKIE TIP

Instead of rolling these in the granulated sugar, roll them in suggested toppings. Try a few different versions, such as some rolled in pistachios, others in cocoa or coconut for a real variety of flavors, colors, and textures.

Sugar Pretzels
Mandelbrezeln, Kringlor

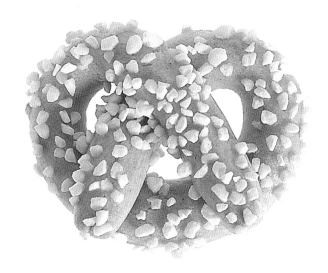

✳ **TYPE** *Shaped cookie*   ✳ **HABITAT** *Germany* (Mandelbrezeln) *and Scandinavia* (Kringlor)

✳ **DESCRIPTION** *This is an elegant, not-too-sweet cookie with a classic white pearl-sugar topping; this kind of sugar looks like the coarse salt that you would use on savory pretzels and can be ordered from King Arthur Flour The Baker's Catalogue (see Resources). Shaping the pretzel might seem difficult, but just read the directions and take it step by step.*

✳ **FIELD NOTES** *Pretzel-shaped cookies are found in Germany as well as in Scandinavia. In fact, in Scandinavia the unique pretzel shape is often used to denote one's profession as a baker. Some have nuts, some don't, but in this recipe the almond extract lends a hint of nut flavor.*

✳ **LIFESPAN** *2 weeks at room temperature in airtight container*

Yield: *100 cookies*

❄ INGREDIENTS

Cookies:
4 cups all-purpose flour
½ teaspoon salt
1 cup (2 sticks) unsalted butter, softened
½ cup granulated sugar
½ teaspoon almond extract
½ teaspoon vanilla extract

2 large eggs
2 large egg yolks

Topping:
1 large egg yolk
1 teaspoon water
White pearl sugar

❄ DIRECTIONS

1. Whisk flour and salt together in a small bowl.

2. In a large bowl with an electric mixer on medium-high speed, beat butter until creamy, about 2 minutes. Add granulated sugar gradually, beating until light and fluffy, about 3 minutes; beat in extracts. Add whole eggs and egg yolks one at a time, beating well after each. Add about one-third of flour mixture and mix on low speed. Gradually add remaining flour, mixing just until blended. Scrape dough onto large piece of plastic wrap. Use wrap to help shape into a large, flat disc, then cover completely with wrap. Refrigerate until firm enough to roll into ropes, at least 1 hour or overnight.

3. Preheat oven to 350 degrees F. Line 2 cookie sheets with parchment paper.

4. Shape dough by rolling about 1 tablespoon at a time beneath your palms on a lightly floured surface into a ¼-inch-diameter rope about 6 inches long, slightly tapering the ends. To form pretzel shape, take one rope and lay it in front of you in a horseshoe shape, open side up. Cross right end over to left end to form a cross about 2 inches down from ends. Now lift both ends and flip them downward, forming the classic pretzel shape. The ends may extend ¼ inch beyond the rounded bottom. Transfer to cookie sheets, placing 2 inches apart.

5. To make topping, whisk together egg yolk and water in a small bowl. Brush each pretzel with egg wash and sprinkle with pearl sugar. Bake until light golden brown, about 25 minutes. Slide parchment onto racks to cool cookies completely.

Thumbprint Cookies

❄ **TYPE** *Shaped and filled cookie*   ❄ **HABITAT** *United States*

❄ **DESCRIPTION** *This is a rich pecan cookie you roll into a ball, roll in extra chopped pecans, and then make a "thumbprint" indentation in the center of each cookie. After baking, you can fill them with jam, lemon curd, or chocolate ganache. Kids seem to have a special affection for them.*

❄ **FIELD NOTES** *Many countries have cookies that involve making an indentation, or thumbprint, which is then filled with jam or other sweet filling. The Austro-Hungarians have* hussaren *cookies, which were named for the buttons on a hussar's military uniform.*

❄ **LIFESPAN** *2 weeks at room temperature in airtight container in single layers separated by waxed paper*

Yield: *64 cookies*

❄ **INGREDIENTS**

Cookies:

2 cups all-purpose flour

½ teaspoon baking powder

½ cup pecan or walnut halves, finely chopped

1 cup (2 sticks) unsalted butter, softened

½ cup granulated sugar

1 teaspoon vanilla extract

1 large egg

Topping:

1¾ cups pecan or walnut halves, finely chopped

Jam, marmalade, lemon curd, or chocolate ganache (page 93, Chocolate Macaroons)

❄ **DIRECTIONS**

1. Whisk flour and baking powder together in a small bowl. Stir in nuts.

2. In a large bowl with an electric mixer on medium-high speed, beat butter until creamy, about 2 minutes. Add sugar gradually, beating until light and fluffy, about 3 minutes; beat in vanilla. Beat in egg. Add about one-third of flour mixture and mix on low speed. Gradually add remaining flour mixture, mixing just until blended. Scrape dough onto a large piece of plastic wrap. Use wrap to help shape into a large, flat disc, then cover completely with wrap. Refrigerate until firm enough to roll into balls, at least 1 hour or overnight.

3. Preheat oven to 350 degrees F. Line 2 cookie sheets with parchment paper.

   Place chopped nuts for topping in a small bowl.

4. Roll dough into 1-inch balls between your lightly floured palms, then roll in chopped nuts to cover completely. Place 2 inches apart on cookie sheets. Make an indentation with your thumb or finger in center of each cookie to make a deep well going about three-quarters of way down into cookie. Bake until very light golden brown and dry to touch, about 15 minutes. They should retain their shape if you lift them to look at bottoms. Place cookie sheets on rack and immediately fill indentations with filling of your choice. Allow to cool completely on sheets.

GOOD COOKIE TIP

These are best filled in one of two ways. Most simply, you can use a teaspoon or a tiny demitasse spoon to help get the filling into the wells. Or you can fill a parchment cone, snip the end to make a ½-inch hole, and pipe in the filling.

Toffee Chocolate Chunk Almond Bars

❋ **TYPE** *Bar cookie*   ❋ **HABITAT** *United States*

❋ **DESCRIPTION** *This brown-sugar bar is jam packed with milk chocolate–covered toffee, dark chocolate chunks, and sliced almonds. There is nothing subtle about it. It is sweet, crunchy, chewy, and chocolatey all at the same time. If you do not want to take the time to chop the chocolate, you can use chocolate chips.*

❋ **FIELD NOTES** *Chocolate-covered toffee candy called buttercrunch is a popular candy to make, eat, and receive at Christmastime; this recipe takes advantage of prepared chocolate-covered toffee candy, but still gives you present-worthy results.*

❋ **LIFESPAN** *4 days at room temperature in airtight container; may also be wrapped in plastic and foil, then put in a zipper-lock plastic freezer bag and frozen for 1 month. Defrost in bag at room temperature.*

Yield: *16 bars*

❄ INGREDIENTS

1 cup all-purpose flour
½ teaspoon baking powder
¼ teaspoon salt
Six 1.4-ounce milk chocolate–covered
    toffee bars (such as Skor or Heath), cut
    into ½-inch pieces
¾ cup bittersweet or semisweet
    chocolate chunks (¼-inch size)

⅓ cup sliced natural almonds
½ cup (1 stick) unsalted butter, melted
½ cup firmly packed light brown sugar
1 teaspoon almond extract
½ teaspoon vanilla extract
1 large egg

❄ DIRECTIONS

1. Preheat oven to 350 degrees F. Coat an 8-inch square baking pan with non-stick spray.

2. Whisk flour, baking powder, and salt together in a small bowl.

3. Toss together toffee chunks, chocolate chunks, and almonds in a small bowl; set aside two portions of the mixture, one measuring 1 cup, the other measuring ½ cup.

4. Whisk together melted butter, brown sugar, and extracts in a medium bowl (or pot you melted the butter in) until blended. Whisk in egg until well combined. Stir in flour mixture until a few streaks of it remain, then stir in largest amount of chocolate-toffee mixture until evenly combined. Spread in an even layer in baking pan and sprinkle top evenly with reserved cup of chocolate-toffee mixture.

5. Bake until light golden brown around edges but still soft in center, about 30 minutes; a toothpick inserted in center should come out with wet batter attached. Sprinkle remaining ½ cup chocolate-toffee mixture evenly over top. Bake until toothpick inserted in center comes out with a few moist crumbs attached, about 5 more minutes. Place pan on rack to cool completely. Cut into 16 bars (4 x 4).

Vanilla Crescents
Vanillen Kipferln

✳ **TYPE** *Shaped cookies*   ✳ **HABITAT** *Austria and Hungary*

✳ **DESCRIPTION** *These delicate, crumbly, crescent-shaped cookies are redolent with vanilla, both from vanilla bean in the batter and in the sugary topping. Make sure to have a vanilla bean on hand; substituting extract just won't give you the same results.*

✳ **FIELD NOTES** *This is a very old recipe, yet still as popular as ever, particularly in Vienna. Indeed, you will occasionally see these called "Viennese" crescents. Vanilla sugar is a classic ingredient in that part of the world, and bakers and even home cooks can find it in grocery stores; lucky for us the technique of this recipe makes it easy to prepare these cookies.*

✳ **LIFESPAN** *2 weeks at room temperature in airtight container*

Yield: *40 crescents*

❄ INGREDIENTS

Cookies:
2 cups all-purpose flour
⅔ cup whole blanched almonds
  (4 ounces)
Pinch of salt
1 cup (2 sticks) unsalted butter, softened
½ moist vanilla bean

¾ cup confectioners' sugar
1 large egg yolk

Topping:
¼ cup granulated sugar
¼ cup confectioners' sugar
½ moist vanilla bean

❄ DIRECTIONS

1. Pulse flour, almonds, and salt together in food processor to coarsely chop nuts, then process until nuts are finely ground.

2. In a large bowl with an electric mixer on medium-high speed, beat butter until creamy, about 2 minutes. Split vanilla bean lengthwise with a sharp knife and scrape seeds into butter using a butter knife or spoon. Beat for 1 minute to blend in seeds. Add confectioners' sugar and beat until light and fluffy, about 3 minutes. Beat in egg yolk. Add about one-third of flour mixture and mix on low speed. Gradually add remaining flour mixture, mixing just until blended. Scrape dough onto large piece of plastic wrap. Use wrap to help shape into a large, flat disc, then cover completely with wrap. Refrigerate until firm enough to roll, at least 1 hour or overnight (in which case you may need it to soften a bit at room temperature before shaping).

3. To make topping, wipe out the food processor to clean it of any flour. Add both sugars. Split vanilla bean lengthwise with a sharp knife and scrape seeds into sugar mixture using a butter knife or spoon. Pulse several times to disperse seeds. Pour vanilla sugar into a small bowl.

4. Preheat oven to 350 degrees F. Line 2 cookie sheets with parchment paper.

5. Roll dough between your palms or on a lightly floured surface into ½-inch-wide x 2½-inch-long logs with slightly tapered ends. Place about 2 inches apart on cookie sheets and bend into a crescent shape. Repeat with remaining dough.

6. Bake until light golden brown around edges and on bottom, about 15 minutes. Slide parchment onto racks to cool cookies for a minute or two. While still warm, roll each cookie in vanilla sugar and return to parchment on rack to cool completely.

Vanilla Sugar Wreaths
Berlinerkranzen

❄ **TYPE** *Piped cookie*   ❄ **HABITAT** *Germany*

❄ **DESCRIPTION** *These buttery cookies are not terribly sweet, which makes them a nice counterpoint to other Christmas treats. The wreaths are formed by piping the soft dough through a pastry bag fitted with a star tip, so make sure you have the right tools on hand.*

❄ **FIELD NOTES** *Similar recipes are found in Germany and Norway. The German word* kranz *means "wreath" or "garland." The addition of the hard-cooked egg is a common component in the various recipes.*

❄ **LIFESPAN** *2 weeks at room temperature in airtight container*

Yield: *36 wreaths*

❄ INGREDIENTS

2¼ cups all-purpose flour
Pinch of salt
1 cup (2 sticks) unsalted butter, softened
½ cup confectioners' sugar, sifted
1 teaspoon vanilla extract

1 large egg yolk
1 large hard-cooked egg yolk, pushed
  through fine mesh sieve
Coarse sugar

❄ DIRECTIONS

1. Line 2 cookie sheets with parchment paper.

2. Whisk flour and salt together in a small bowl.

3. In a large bowl with an electric mixer on medium-high speed, beat butter until creamy, about 2 minutes. Add confectioners' sugar gradually, beating until light and fluffy, about 3 minutes; beat in vanilla. Add egg yolks one at a time, beating well after each. Add about one-third of flour mixture and mix on low speed. Gradually add remaining flour, mixing just until blended. Scrape dough into pastry bag fitted with large star tip (such as Ateco #824 or #864). Pipe wreath-shaped cookies 2 inches apart on cookie sheets. Sprinkle with coarse sugar, taking care not to get too much on the sheet. Refrigerate for 30 minutes.

4. Preheat oven to 350 degrees F. Bake just until light golden brown around edges, about 13 minutes. Slide parchment onto racks to cool the cookies completely.

White Christmas White Chocolate Cranberry Oatmeal Cookies

✳ **TYPE** *Drop cookie*   ✳ **HABITAT** *United States*

✳ **DESCRIPTION** *These oatmeal cookies are extra chewy due to the melted butter; the browning of the butter gives them a very rich flavor. With chopped white chocolate and dried cranberries thrown in the mix, you've never tasted oatmeal cookies like this before.*

✳ **FIELD NOTES** *I made these up from scratch, so their birthdate is summer 2002, in Amherst, Massachusetts! Oatmeal cookies are all-American and dried cranberries can now be found in most any supermarket, so these are a quintessentially American cookie.*

✳ **RELATED SPECIES** Dark Chocolate Cherry Oatmeal Cookies: *Substitute dark chocolate for the white and dried cherries for cranberries;* Browned Butter Oatmeal Cookies with Milk Chocolate and Candied Orange: *Substitute milk chocolate for the white and diced candied orange for cranberries.*

✳ **LIFESPAN** *1 week at room temperature in airtight container*

Yield: *75 cookies*

❄ INGREDIENTS

2⅔ cups rolled oats (use old-fashioned, not quick or instant)

1½ cups all-purpose flour

1 teaspoon baking soda

½ teaspoon salt

1 cup dried cranberries

6 ounces white chocolate, broken into pieces

½ cup walnut halves, finely chopped

1 cup (2 sticks) unsalted butter

1⅓ cups firmly packed light brown sugar

1 teaspoon ground cinnamon

2 large eggs

1 teaspoon vanilla extract

❄ DIRECTIONS

1. Preheat oven to 350 degrees F. Line 2 cookie sheets with parchment paper.

2. Whisk oats, flour, baking soda, and salt together in a medium bowl; stir in dried cranberries, white chocolate, and nuts.

3. In a medium saucepan, melt butter over medium heat. Continue to simmer over medium-low heat until the milk solids turn golden brown, about 4 minutes; take care not to burn.

4. Pour browned butter into a large bowl and whisk in brown sugar until combined. Whisk in cinnamon, then whisk in eggs and vanilla, beating well after each. Add dry mixture to wet ingredients and stir just until combined. Mixture will be thick. Drop by generously rounded tablespoon 2 inches apart onto cookie sheets.

5. Bake until light golden brown and just dry to the touch, but still a little soft inside, about 10 minutes. Slide parchment onto racks to cool cookies completely.

GOOD COOKIE TIP

For chewier oatmeal cookies, bake 30 seconds to 1 minute less. For very crispy cookies, bake 30 seconds to 1 minute more.

Yuletide Mocha Orange Patchwork, Pinwheel, and Marbled Cookies

✳ **TYPE** *Rolled cookie*   ✳ **HABITAT** *United States*

✳ **DESCRIPTION** *Don't be put off by the length of this recipe. Taken step by step, it is really very easy. It starts with an orange sugar cookie dough and a chocolate-coffee (mocha) sugar cookie dough, and then the fun begins! You can layer and roll them for eye-catching spirals or cut out shapes within shapes to create two-toned patchwork cookies. Gently knead together scraps of both flavors to make marbled cookies. Tip: Use half the dough for spirals, half for patchwork cookies, and all of the scraps for marbled cookies. You will get three very different-looking cookies from one recipe.*

✳ **RELATED SPECIES** *One of my 12-year-old twins, Forrester, made* Mocha Peanut Butter Calzones—*not exactly Christmasy, I know, but really delicious nonetheless. Roll out the mocha dough and cut into 2-inch rounds. Place ½ teaspoon creamy hydrogenated (not natural) peanut butter on half of each round. Fold over other half to make a half-moon shape and crimp edges together with fork to seal. Place 2 inches apart on cookie sheets and bake, then cool and store as directed above.*

✳ **LIFESPAN** *2 weeks at room temperature in airtight container*

Yield: *100 pinwheels or 50 assorted 3- to 4-inch patchwork cookies; yield of marbled cookies varies*

❊ INGREDIENTS

Orange dough:

3 cups all-purpose flour
½ teaspoon baking soda
¼ teaspoon salt
1 cup (2 sticks) unsalted butter, softened
1 cup granulated sugar
2 teaspoons finely grated orange zest
1 teaspoon vanilla extract
1 large egg

Mocha dough:

2½ cups all-purpose flour
½ cup Dutch-processed unsweetened cocoa powder
½ teaspoon baking soda
¼ teaspoon salt
1 cup (2 sticks) unsalted butter, softened
1 cup granulated sugar
1 teaspoon instant espresso or coffee powder
1 teaspoon vanilla extract
1 large egg

❊ DIRECTIONS

1. For orange dough, whisk flour, baking soda, and salt together in a small bowl.

   In a large bowl with an electric mixer on medium-high speed, beat butter until creamy, about 2 minutes. Add sugar gradually, beating until light and fluffy, about 3 minutes; beat in orange zest and vanilla. Beat in egg. Add about one-third of flour mixture and mix on low speed. Gradually add remaining flour, mixing just until blended. Scrape dough onto large piece of plastic wrap. Use wrap to help shape into a large, flat disc, then cover completely with wrap. Refrigerate until firm enough to roll out, at least 2 hours or overnight.

2. For mocha dough, whisk flour, cocoa, baking soda, and salt together in a small bowl. In a large bowl with an electric mixer on medium-high speed, beat butter until creamy, about 2 minutes. Add sugar gradually, beating until light and fluffy, about 3 minutes. Dissolve instant espresso in vanilla, then beat into dough. Beat in egg. Add about one-third of flour mixture and mix on low speed. Gradually add remaining flour, mixing just until blended. Scrape dough onto large piece of plastic wrap. Use wrap to help shape into a large, flat disc, then cover completely with wrap. Refrigerate until firm enough to roll, at least 2 hours or overnight.

3. Line 2 cookie sheets with parchment paper.

4. *For Patchwork Cookies:* Choose two compatible cookie cutters, large and small, such as a large and small star or bell or a large gingerbread person and a small heart. The only absolute is that the small cookie cutter must fit within the larger one with a border of dough all around. Roll both doughs out to ¼-inch thickness on lightly floured surface. I will use stars as our example: Cut out a large orange star and place on cookie sheet. Cut out a large mocha

star and place 2 inches away on same sheet. Now cut a small orange star out of the larger orange star and a small mocha star out of the large mocha star. Place small mocha star inside large orange star (in void created by removing small star) and small orange star inside large mocha star (see photograph above). Be as creative as you like, but keep similarly sized cookies on same sheet for even baking times. When pan is filled with cookies, place in freezer for 15 minutes or refrigerator for 30 minutes.

For Pinwheel Cookies: Cut each flavored dough in half. Roll half of orange dough out to ¼-inch thickness on lightly floured surface to a rectangle about 14 x 16 inches. Roll half of mocha dough out in the same manner. Place orange dough on top of mocha dough and square off the four sides by trimming with a pizza cutter or sharp knife. Starting at one short end, roll both doughs up together as tightly as possible. Your roll should be about 2 inches in diameter. Carefully cover rolled dough with plastic wrap. Repeat with remaining dough halves. Freeze 30 minutes or refrigerate for 1 hour, until very firm. (Rolls may be frozen at this point for up to 1 month.) Trim ends of roll so that spiral design is flat. Cut ¼-inch-thick slices off roll and place 2 inches apart on cookie sheets.

For Marbled Cookies: Briefly knead all the scraps left from both flavors of dough together to create a marbled effect, roll out as described above, and cut out cookies as you wish; they will look marbled.

5. Preheat oven to 350 degrees F. Bake until dry to touch and edges are just beginning to color, about 12 minutes for cookies 2 inches across. Lift up a cookie; it should lift without breaking, and bottom will be slightly colored. Adjust baking time up or down accordingly if cookies are much smaller or larger. Slide parchment onto racks to cool cookies completely.

Resources

Beryl's Cake Decorating and Pastry Supplies
P.O. Box 1584
North Springfield, VA 22151
(703) 256-6951 or
(800) 488-2749
FAX (703) 750-3779
www.beryls.com
Beryl herself answers the phone and provides highly personal and professional customer service. She offers cutters of all sorts, food colors, pans, pastry bags and decorating tips, books, and more. Catalog available.

Blue Magic
The Luce Corporation
336 Putnam Avenue
P.O. Box 4124
Hamden, CT 06514
(203) 787-0281
Blue Magic moisture absorbers are small devices that keep crisp cookies crisp (see page 17 for a full description). Call for catalog and order form.

The Chef's Catalog
3215 Commercial Avenue
Northbrook, IL 60062-1900
(800) 338-3232
www.chefscatalog.com
Great mail-order catalog through which you can buy KitchenAid mixers, large professional-sized rubber spatulas, extra long oven mitts, parchment paper, and more. And all at very competitive prices.

Chocosphere
(877) 99-CHOCO
FAX (877) 912-4626
www.chocosphere.com
This Internet-only company specializes in high-quality chocolates from more than a dozen sources that are great to eat and wonderful to melt or cut into chunks for your cookies. Owner Jerry Kryszek offers excellent personal service, and they ship nationwide. If you are not online, you can call in your order.

Hammersong
221 South Potomac Street
Boonsboro, MD 21713
(301) 432-4320
This company handcrafts the most exquisite cookie cutters. They have such detail that not much decoration is needed, but if you do want to frost and embellish your cookies, the details of the cutter will give you guidelines, which will make your job much easier. Any which way, your cookies will be extraordinarily beautiful. Owner Bill Cukla will give you personal service. Call for a catalog (there is a $3 charge).

The House on the Hill, Inc.
P.O. Box 7003
Villa Park, IL 60181
(630) 969-2624
FAX (630) 969-2615
info@houseonthehill.net or
www.houseonthehill.net
This company has a great Web site where you can learn everything you want to know about springerle cookies, as well as some others, such as *speculaas*. Peruse the site for dozens of antique reproduction molds, as well as for books and tools related to baking these unique cookies. Catalog available.

King Arthur Flour The Baker's Catalogue
P.O. Box 876
Norwich, VT 05055
(800) 827-6836
FAX (802) 649-5359
www.kingarthurflour.com
This frequently updated catalog has flours of all description, vanillas, chocolates, candied fruit and citrus rinds, pearl sugar and coarse sugar, scales, high-quality measuring cups, including ones in odd sizes, and more. They have small ice cream scoops that make baking cookies quick and easy.

KitchenAid
P.O. Box 218
St. Joseph, MI 49085
(800) 541-6390
www.kitchenaid.com
Go directly to this Web site for a complete listing of their high-quality products. All of my cookies were tested in a KitchenAid oven and made with a KitchenAid mixer. I bought my mixer almost 20 years ago, and it is still going strong; this is a worthwhile investment for any avid baker.

Kitchen Arts and Letters
1435 Lexington Avenue
New York, NY 10128
(212) 876-5550
FAX (212) 876-3584
This is a cookbook lover's dream store. It is a small shop that is filled to the brim with cookbooks new and old, in print, out-of-print, foreign and domestic, texts for the professional, and as many books on baking as you could ever want. Not only do

they probably have the books you need, but if they don't, they can probably find them. And (this is the best part) the staff is extremely knowledgeable about food. You can call up and ask a culinary question and get an answer quite promptly. Use this gem of a resource and by all means visit the store itself when in Manhattan.

La Cuisine
323 Cameron Street
Alexandria, VA 22314
(703) 836-4435 or
(800) 521-1176
FAX (703) 836-8925
www.lacuisineus.com
This very comprehensive supply house has excellent equipment, such as cookie sheet pans, springerle molds, and a wonderful line of cookie cutters made by a company called Hammersong, which are extremely detailed. They also have high-quality ingredients, such as chocolates and vanilla beans. Catalog available.

New York Cake and Baking Distributors
56 West 22nd Street
New York, NY 10010
(212) 675-2253 or
(800) 942-2539
www.nycakesupplies.com
You can shop here for a huge variety of colored sugars in many textures, food colors, pastry bags and decorating tips, nonpareils, cookie sheets, parchment paper, cookie cutters, and more.

Penzeys Spices
P.O. Box 993
W19362 Apollo Drive
Muskego, WI 53150
(800) 741-7787
www.penzeys.com
This company has an amazing array of fresh herbs and spices. Check them out for excellent cinnamon, nutmeg, ginger (both ground and crystallized), cardamom, cocoa, vanilla beans, and extracts, among other ingredients. Catalog available.

Sur La Table
Pike Place Farmers Market
84 Pine Street
Seattle, WA 98101
(206) 448-2244 or
(800) 243-0852
www.surlatable.com
Here you will find pans, pastry bags and decorating tips, rolling pins, high-quality cookie-sheet pans, spatulas, and more. Catalog available.

Sweet Celebrations/Maid of Scandinavia
7009 Washington Avenue
*   South*
Edina, MN 55439
(800) 328-6722
www.sweetc.com or
www.maidofscandinavia.com
This company used to be called Maid of Scandinavia; now it is called Sweet Celebrations. They have an extensive line of equipment including more cookie cutters than you could ever imagine, pastry bags and decorating tips, decorator's combs, spritz cookie presses, cookie sheet pans, chocolates, colored sug-

ars, coarse sugar, nonpareils, the Brown Sugar Bear to keep your soft cookies and brown sugar soft, and more. This is where I bought my VillaWare *pizzelle* and *krumkake* machines. Catalog available.

Williams-Sonoma
P.O. Box 7456
San Francisco, CA 94120
(415) 421-4242 or
(800) 541-2233
FAX (415) 421-5253
www.williams-sonoma.com
Famous for their mail-order catalog, they also have stores nationwide. You will find well-made, accurate measuring tools, KitchenAid mixers, spritz cookie makers, vanilla extract, some chocolate and cocoa, and other baking equipment, including pans and spatulas of all sorts. Around the Christmas holiday their catalog features gorgeous packing materials for your baked goods, like ribbons, monogrammed boxes, and more.

Wilton Industries, Inc.
2240 West 75th Street
Woodbridge, IL 60517
(708) 963-7100 or
(800) 794-5866
www.wilton.com
Great catalog with heavy-duty pans, cookie sheets, pastry bags and decorating tips, spritz cookie presses, food colors, cookie cutters, decorator's combs, parchment paper, chocolates, cocoa, colored sugars, and much more.

Index